Women of Ancient Rome

Titles in the Women in History series include:

WOMEN
IN
HISTORY

Women of Ancient Rome

Don Nardo

LUCENT
BOOKS®

THOMSON

GALE

San Diego • Detroit • New York • San Francisco • Cleveland • New Haven, Conn. • Waterville, Maine • London • Munich

THOMSON

─────✳─────™

GALE

© 2003 by Lucent Books. Lucent Books is an imprint of The Gale Group, Inc.,
a division of Thomson Learning, Inc.

Lucent Books® and Thomson Learning™ are trademarks used herein under license.

For more information, contact
Lucent Books
27500 Drake Rd.
Farmington Hills, MI 48331-3535
Or you can visit our Internet site at http://www.gale.com

LIBRARY OF CONGRESS CATALOGING-IN-PUBLICATION DATA
Nardo, Don, 1947–
Women of ancient Rome / by Don Nardo.
p. cm. — (Women in history series)
Summary: Discusses fact, fictions, status, occupations, love, marriage, divorce,
habits, personal lives, economic and social status, and influence on the women
of ancient Rome.
ISBN 1-59018-169-7 (hardback : alk. paper)
1. Women—Rome—History—Juvenile literature. 2. Women—History—
To 500—Juvenile literature. I. Title. II. Series.
HQ1136 .N37 2003
305.4 '09376—dc21
2002001392

Printed in the United States of America

Contents

Foreword

The story of the past as told in traditional historical writings all too often leaves the impression that if men are not the only actors in the narrative, they are assuredly the main characters. With a few notable exceptions, males were the political, military, and economic leaders in virtually every culture throughout recorded time. Since traditional historical scholarship focuses on the public arenas of government, foreign relations, and commerce, the actions and ideas of men—or at least of powerful men—are naturally at the center of conventional accounts of the past.

In the last several decades, however, many historians have abandoned their predecessors' emphasis on "great men" to explore the past "from the bottom up," a phenomenon that has had important consequences for the study of women's history. These social historians, as they are known, focus on the day-to-day experiences of the "silent majority"—those people typically omitted from conventional scholarship because they held relatively little political or economic sway within their societies. In the new social history, members of ethnic and racial minorities, factory workers, peasants, slaves, children, and women are no longer relegated to the background but are placed at the very heart of the narrative.

Around the same time social historians began broadening their research to include women and other previously neglected elements of society, the feminist movement of the late 1960s and 1970s was also bringing unprecedented attention to the female heritage. Feminists hoped that by examining women's past experiences, contemporary women could better understand why and how gender-based expectations had developed in their societies, as well as how they might reshape inherited—and typically restrictive—economic, social, and political roles in the future.

Today, some four decades after the feminist and social history movements gave new impetus to the study of women's history, there is a rich and continually growing body of work on all aspects of women's lives in the past. The Lucent Books Women in History series draws upon this abundant and diverse literature to introduce students to women's experiences within a variety of past cultures and time periods in terms of the distinct roles they filled. In their capacities as workers, activists, and artists, women excerted significant influence on important events whether they conformed to or broke from traditional roles. The women in History titles depict extraordinary women who managed to attain positions of influence in their male-dominated societies, including such celebrated heroines as the feisty medieval queen Eleanor of Aquitaine, the brilliant propagandist of the American Revolution Mercy Otis Warren, and the courageous African American activist of the Civil War era, Harriet Tubman. Included as well are the stories of the ordinary—and often overlooked—women of the past who also helped shape their societies in myriad ways—moral, intellectual, and economic—without straying far from customary gender roles: the housewives and mothers, school teachers and church volunteers, midwives and nurses and wartime camp followers.

In this series, readers will discover that many of these unsung women took more significant parts in the great political and social upheavals of their day than has often been recognized. In *Women of the American Revolution,* for example, students will learn how American housewives assumed a crucial role in helping the Patriots win the war against Britain. They accomplished this by planting and harvesting fields, producing and trading goods, and doing whatever else was necessary to maintain the family farm or business in the absence of their soldier husbands despite the heavy burden of housekeeping and child care duties they already bore. By their self-sacrificing actions, competence, and ingenuity, these anonymous heroines not only kept their families alive, but kept the economy of their struggling young nation going as well during eight long years of war.

Each volume in this series contains generous commentary from the works of respected contemporary scholars, but the Women in History series particularly emphasizes quotations from primary sources such as diaries, letters, and journals whenever possible to allow the women of the past to speak for themselves. These first-hand accounts not only help students to better understand the dimensions of women's daily spheres—the work they did, the organizations they belonged to, the physical hardships they faced—but also how they viewed themselves and their actions in the light of their society's expectations for their sex.

The distinguished American historian Mary Beard once wrote that women have always been a "force in history." It is hoped that the books in this series will help students to better appreciate the vital yet often little known ways in which women of the past have shaped their societies and cultures.

Introduction:
Roman Society's
Unsung Heroes

The story of ancient Roman women is a rich and fascinating facet of the greater saga of Rome itself. Roman civilization was dominated and run almost entirely by men. Although women made a number of important social and legal advances over the years, gaining considerable emancipation, they never acquired the rights to vote and hold public office. Nevertheless, the role of women in Roman society was far from minor. Without mothers, wives, daughters, priestesses, and female slaves and workers, the efforts of the men would have been severely diminished.

Indeed, even though Roman men rarely acknowledged the importance and contributions of their women, the latter were often unsung heroes who kept society running on an even keel. "During wars or political purges," scholars Marjorie and Benjamin Lightman point out,

> when fighting men left the city, women stayed. They coped with the inflation in costs [caused by wars], the protection of the family's property, and the problems of securing food. When

wars did not go well, they defended the city's walls and hid their wealth and children from the victors. They also became slaves of the victors and the greater number of refugees from slaughter. If lucky, they lived long enough after defeat to avenge their men, sometimes through revolutions and other times through the law courts. In the aftermath of civil wars, which were especially devastating for the elite, it often fell to mothers, daughters, sisters, and former sisters-in-law to rear, dower, and arrange the marriages of orphaned children who reestablished stability and re-created bloodlines from the past.[1]

Women played these vital kinds of roles throughout Rome's history and thereby helped to make that history as extraordinarily long as it was. The traditional founding date of Rome, as calculated by Roman scholars in the first century B.C., is 753 B.C., although the so-called seven hills of Rome were likely occupied for at least two or three centuries prior to that date. The

Roman Monarchy, the government and era in which kings ruled, lasted until 509 B.C., when the leading landholders threw out the last king and established the Republic. This representative form of government, dominated by the Senate, endured until the last decades of the first century B.C. At that time Octavian, the victor of the last of a series of terrible civil wars, took the title of Augustus ("the revered one") and established the Roman Empire, an autocratic realm that lasted until A.D. 476.

During all these centuries, Roman women gave birth to and raised sons to run the state and fight the wars; at times advised powerful sons or husbands behind the scenes; maintained the flame burning in the state hearth and played key roles in religious festivals; organized and ran households across the realm; shopped and traded in marketplaces; labored in numerous professions, including some considered exclusively male; often learned to read and write, and in some cases wrote prose and poetry; and occupied numerous other vital niches in society's fabric.

The Nature of the Evidence

Modern historians know that Roman women did these things thanks to the surviving evidence, some of it literary, some archaeological. Unfortunately, though, the picture of Roman women painted in the literary sources remains incomplete and

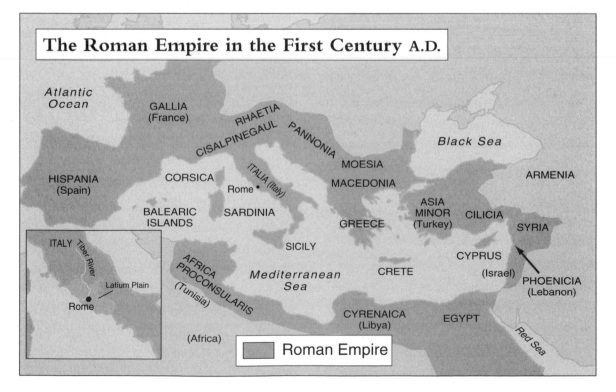

The Roman Empire in the First Century A.D.

often unclear. This stems from two short-comings of these sources, the first being that the vast majority were not written by women and therefore do not constitute direct testimony. As Hunter College scholar Sarah Pomeroy puts it,

> The literary testimony presents grave problems for the social historian. Women pervade nearly every genre of classical [ancient Greek and Roman] literature, yet often the bias of the author distorts the information. Aside from some scraps of lyric poetry, the extant [surviving] formal literature of classical antiquity was all written by men. In addition, misogyny [contempt for or dislike of women] taints much ancient literature [since most men, including the writers, believed women were fundamentally inferior to men].[2]

The other problem is that most of the surviving evidence describes the lives of upper-class women, even though they made up only a small fraction of the female population. "Ancient history, to a considerable degree, has been basically the study of the ruling classes," says Pomeroy.

> The women who are known to us from the formal literature of antiquity are mainly those who belonged to or associated with the wealthy or intellectually elite groups of society. It must

also be recognized that there is more information available on women who were famous—whether for good or evil.[3]

Scholars must therefore be very careful and critical in examining the ancient male-written sources available about Roman women. Among others, these sources include the works of the Roman historians Livy (first century B.C.), Tacitus (first century A.D.), and Suetonius (second century A.D.); the great orator Cicero (first century B.C.); the poets Virgil, Ovid, and Catullus (first century B.C.); the urbane philosopher Seneca (first century A.D.); the prolific letter writer Pliny the Younger (first century A.D.); the bitter satirist Juvenal (first to second century A.D.); and the Greek biographer Plutarch (first century A.D.). In addition, the surviving commentary and opinions of male jurists shed some light on women's lives by showing how the law defined female status and rights at various times in Roman history.

To supplement these written sources, scholars turn to the surviving archaeological evidence. This includes depictions of women in sculpture, vase and wall paintings, mosaics, and on coins; tombstone epitaphs and other inscriptions, such as graffiti on the walls of buildings (especially at Pompeii, a Roman city buried and largely preserved by the eruption of Mt. Vesuvius in A.D. 79); personal artifacts such

The women of a wealthy Roman household welcome home the master of the house. Most of the surviving literary evidence describes upper-class women.

as jewelry, grooming items, kitchen utensils, looms, and so forth; and scraps of papyrus (a kind of paper) containing fragments of letters, prayers, and marriage contracts and other legal documents pertaining to women (mostly from the Roman province of Egypt). According to scholars Diana Kleiner and Susan Matheson,

> Material remains from ancient Rome have preserved valuable evidence for the appearance and accomplishments of Roman women. . . . Each one of

these [forms of evidence] narrates part of the story left by an ambitious empress, an innocent princess, an aristocrat . . . a well-placed priestess, a gifted poetess, a solid middle-class tavern owner, a popular midwife, and a fetching concubine [mistress].[4]

In this way, modern researchers attempt to piece together the lives of women whose voices have been stilled not only by death but also by the sad loss to posterity of their own words, views, and feelings.

Chapter 1:
Early Roman Women: Legend Versus Fact

From the dawn of Rome's epic rise to power over the Mediterranean world comes the story of one of the first fondly remembered Roman heroines. Veturia was the mother of Coriolanus, a leading Roman general. Feeling he had been mistreated by his own people, Coriolanus defected to the land of an Italian enemy, the Volscians, and soon marched on Rome at the head of a Volscian army. According to Livy, Veturia was upset and indignant. She visited her son's camp and when he tried to greet her with a kiss she stopped him and said sternly:

> I would know before I accept your kiss whether I have come to an enemy or to a son, whether I am here as your mother or as a prisoner of war. Have my long life and unhappy old age brought me to this, that I should see you first in exile, then the enemy of your country? Had you the heart to ravage the earth which bore and bred you? When Rome was before your eyes, did not the thought come to you "within those walls is

my home, with the gods that watch over it—and my mother and my wife and my children"?[5]

Shamed by his mother, and by similar words from his wife, Coriolanus withdrew, refusing to attack his native city (and later met death at the hands of the Volscians). Rome was saved, and the course of history changed by women who seem to have commanded much respect and moral authority in Roman society.

This at least was the way Livy portrayed some of Rome's early women. The problem is that Livy lived long after the era in question, as Princeton University scholar Elaine Fantham explains:

> Romanticizing legends like this became part of Roman patriotic tradition just because Roman society was so late in producing its own literature; the first known dramatic and epic poets come five hundred years after the legendary founding of the city. . . . So the legendary traditions about queens and other women of

early Rome were shaped by writers of a later age.[6]

In fact, no written sources and very little other evidence for Roman women and their lives survives from before the third century B.C., when the Romans began writing about their history. And nothing substantial was composed until the first century B.C., the age of Livy, Cicero, Virgil, and Ovid. But by that time it was no longer possible to separate fact from legend.

It is certainly possible, and even probable, that some of the legends about early Rome were based on real characters and events. The famous Romulus, the legendary founder and namesake of Rome, for example, may well have been the city's first king. The question is how much of his colorful story, including the parts dealing with women, was real, how much exaggerated, and how much completely fabricated? Unfortunately, Livy and his colleagues, who wrote about Romulus many centuries later, rarely, if ever, asked these critical questions. Their main motivation in telling such tales was

In this painting by nineteenth-century Italian artist Raffaele Postiglione, Veturia scolds Coriolanus for abandoning his home and family.

not to present a strictly accurate historical account. Instead, says Fantham, these men were

> motivated by the need to represent a Roman past [that was] heroic and virtuous. . . . In the edifying exemplary tales of Cicero and the idealizing narrative of Virgil, Livy, or Ovid, the early Romans succeeded through moral excellence, and their wives and mothers raised their voices only like Veturia, to remind their menfolk of their duty to the country.[7]

Because so little is known about the lives of women in Rome's first five centuries, these moralistic legends are all that historians have to go on and therefore must be considered. The hope persists that ongoing and future archaeological discoveries will either support or call into question the events they describe.

Capture of the Sabine Women

The first time women are mentioned in Roman legend they are conspicuous because of their absence. For an unspecified time after Romulus had established the city of Rome, almost all of those who initially settled there were men, and they had difficulty obtaining brides. Clearly, they could not hope to build a growing, thriving society without women. To solve this problem, Romulus came up with an audacious plan. He invited the residents of a number of neighboring towns, all inhab-

Social Status Reflected in Names

To some extent, the changing status of Roman women was reflected in their names. In the Monarchy and first years of the Republic, free men and women generally had two names—their nomen and praenomen. The nomen was the name of a person's clan, which was often a measure of social rank and status. The praenomen, or first name, identified the individual. Over time, the custom of giving women two names was discontinued, and for the rest of republican times most young girls went by a feminine form of the father's nomen. Thus, Gaius Julius Caesar's daughter was called Julia, and Marcus Tullius Cicero's daughter was known as Tullia. Later, however, in the Empire, when women's social status had increased, many women once again used two names, and sometimes even three (the *tria nomina,* consisting not only of the praenomen and nomen but also the cognomen, denoting an individual family within a clan).

A nineteenth-century engraving depicts the abduction of the Sabine women by Romulus and the other Roman men. The event ignited a short but bloody war.

ited by a Latin people called the Sabines, to a great religious festival where athletic games and theatrical performances would be staged. His real intention, however, was not to foster friendship but to steal the Sabine women. "On the appointed day," Livy wrote,

> crowds flocked to Rome, partly, no doubt, out of sheer curiosity to see

the new town. . . . All the Sabines were there . . . with their wives and children. . . . Then the great moment came; the show began, and nobody had eyes or thought for anything else. This was the Romans' opportunity. At a given signal, all the able-bodied men burst through the crowd and seized the young women. Most of the girls were the prize of whoever got

Ovid on the Sabine Women

Livy was not the only first-century-B.C. Roman writer who described the abduction of the Sabine women. This is the poet Ovid's more playful account (from Ovid's *Love Poems*).

> The king [Romulus] gave the sign for which they'd so eagerly watched. Project Rape was on. Up they sprang then with a lusty roar, [and] laid hot hands on the girls. As timorous doves flee eagles, as lambkin runs wild when it sees the hated wolf, so this wild charge of men left the girls all panic-stricken. Not one had the same color in her cheek as before. The

> same nightmare for all, though terror's features varied: Some tore their hair, some just froze where they sat; some, dismayed, kept silence, others vainly yelled for Mamma; some wailed; some gaped; some fled, some just stood there. So they were carried off as marriage bed plunder. Even so, many contrived to make panic look fetching. Any girl who resisted her pursuer too vigorously would find herself picked up and borne off regardless. "Why spoil those pretty eyes with weeping?" She'd hear, "I'll be all to you that your Dad ever was to your Mum."

> hold of them first. But a few conspicuously handsome ones had been previously marked down by leading senators, and these were brought to their houses by special gangs. . . . By this act of violence, the fun of the festival broke up in panic. The girls' unfortunate parents made good their escape, not without bitter comments on the treachery of their hosts. . . . The young women were no less indignant and full of foreboding about the future.[8]

But Romulus assured the captured brides that they would be well treated and tried to talk them into accepting their new situation.

Soon, however, the male Sabines reorganized and attacked Rome in an effort to win back their women. Romulus and his troops managed to defeat the first several groups that marched on the city. But the Sabines of the city of Cures, led by their king, Titus Tatius, were able to surround Rome. A great battle occurred, and many on both sides were killed before the former Sabine women rushed out and demanded a truce. They could not simply stand by, they declared, and watch their fathers, brothers, and new husbands slaughter one another. The result was a treaty in which the two sides agreed to merge as one people, with Romulus and Titus Tatius as joint rulers. Rome had made its first conquest and absorption of a neighboring people, opening the way for the newly founded city's spectacular rise to greatness.

The most striking aspect of this story is the influence and moral authority the women wielded over the men. Although they were physically too weak to resist capture and forced marriage, as a group the women exerted extraordinary power in halting a major armed conflict. Moreover, this incident is only the first of many in early Roman history in which Rome's women are directly involved in stopping a war or otherwise helping to decide the course of political affairs. The story of Coriolanus's indignant mother, Veturia, who saved Rome from a Volscian invasion, is another.

Symbols of Female Virtue and Bravery

Still another such example, one later Romans viewed as a critical event in their proud history, involved Lucretia, whose mistreatment and heroism led to the establishment of the Roman Republic. She was the wife of an aristocrat and patriot named L. Tarquinius Collatinus. In 509 B.C., according to the story, the widely disliked son of the equally hated King Tarquinius Superbus raped Lucretia. Afterward, she summoned her husband, along with her uncle, Lucius Junius Brutus, and in Livy's words:

They found Lucretia sitting in her room, in deep distress. Tears rose to her eyes as they entered, and to her husband's question, "Is it well with you?" she answered, "No. What can be well with a woman who has lost her honor? In your bed, Collatinus, is the impress of another man. My body only has been violated. My heart is

The king's son, Sextus Tarquinius, prepares to assault the virtuous Lucretia.

innocent, and death will be my witness. Give me your solemn promise that the adulterer shall be punished—he is Sextus Tarquinius. He it is who last night came as my enemy disguised as my guest, and took his pleasure of me. That pleasure will be my death—and his, too, if you are men." The promise [to punish the rapist] was given. . . . They tried to comfort her. They told her she was helpless, and therefore innocent; that he alone was guilty. It was the mind, they said, that sinned, not the body. Without intention there could never be guilt. "What is due *him*," Lucretia said, "is for you to decide. As for me, I am innocent of fault, but I will take my punishment. Never shall Lucretia provide a precedent for unchaste women to escape what they deserve." With these words she drew a knife from under her robe, drove it into her heart, and fell forward, dead. [9]

Seeing the rape and death of Lucretia as yet another of the Monarchy's long list of abuses, Brutus, Collatinus, and other leading citizens led a revolution that ousted the royal family and founded a republican form of government.

No one knows how much of this tale is true. Even Livy did not know for sure, since he lived almost five hundred years after the fact. It may well be that the rape of the

daughter of a nobleman was the spark that ignited the republican revolution. By Livy's time, however, Lucretia had also become a symbolic figure. Her suicidal sacrifice, though tragic, was widely seen as proper, an example set for Romans through the ages of female virtue at its best. According to traditional social mores, sexual fidelity (*pudicitia*) to her husband was a Roman woman's primary moral duty. By Livy's day, infidelity was not uncommon, and women did not commit suicide to atone for it. But society still frowned on it, no matter what the circumstances. And Lucretia remained an ideal woman in Roman lore.

A Roman heroine of a different sort appears in another legend from the early days of the Republic. Shortly after the new government had been established, an Etruscan king, Lars Porsenna, ruler of the city-state of Clusium, attacked Rome. When he failed to conquer it, he made a deal with Roman leaders. In exchange for the return of the Janiculum Hill (across the Tiber River from Rome), which he had managed to capture, Porsenna received several Roman hostages, including a young woman named Cloelia. Not long after her capture, Cloelia hatched a plot to free herself and some of the other hostages. They managed to swim back across the river to Rome. Porsenna was so impressed with Cloelia's courage that he eventually gave up trying to get her back and even freed some of the remaining hostages in her honor.

For her unselfishness and bravery, the Romans later honored Cloelia with a public statue, an honor accorded very few women in Rome. What is more, the statue depicted her wearing a toga and riding atop a horse in the pose of a military commander, both normally seen as male honors. Writing in the first century A.D., the noted scholar and encyclopedist Pliny the Elder described it this way:

> [Such male] distinction was actually extended to women with the equestrian statue of Cloelia, as if it were not enough for her to be clad in a toga, although statues were not voted to Lucretia and to Brutus who had driven out the kings.[10]

As Lucretia became a symbol of female virtue, Cloelia came to represent women's bravery and patriotism.

Etruscan Women's Liberation?

Such legends reveal mainly what later Roman men envisioned as the female ideal in "the good old days" of early Rome. Obviously missing or unclear in such stories is vital information about the status and everyday lives of real Roman women in the Monarchy and early Republic. Another source of information about these women, one indirect but based more on evidence than legend, comes from studies of Italy's early Etruscan and Greek women. The Etruscans were a culturally advanced peo-

This seventeenth-century French painting shows Cloelia leading the hostages to safety.

ple who inhabited the northern half of Italy, including Etruria (the area immediately north of Rome), during much of the first millennium B.C. Another advanced people, the Greeks, established cities in southern Italy in the eighth and seventh centuries B.C., when Rome was still a crude farming community. Both of these peoples exerted significant cultural influences over Rome during its formative years. And both peoples, including their women, were eventually absorbed into the Roman melting pot after Rome conquered them. So, Roman women and society's treatment of them could not help but be influenced to some degree by Etruscan and Greek women.

The reasons for Etruscan influence on Rome are not hard to fathom. Several populous, wealthy, and vibrant independent Etruscan cities existed within one or two days' march from Rome. One or more of these cities fought the more culturally backward and conservative Romans off and on from the seventh to fourth centuries B.C.

Even in times of peace, the Romans were strongly affected by these colorful and often intimidating neighbors. Some of Rome's kings, including the last, Tarquinius Superbus, were Etruscans (though they seem to have gained their powerful positions through personal merit rather than by conquest). These men brought their female relatives with them, naturally, along with various artistic refinements of Etruscan nobility. As scholar Larissa Warren writes,

> The Etruscans' wealth and freedom brought home to the Romans their first experience of civilization and

A stunning terra-cotta portrait of a married couple graces the top of an Etruscan sarcophagus dating to circa 520 B.C. Etruscan women enjoyed high social status.

Tarpeia: Traitor or Hero?

❦

Roman legend maintains that the Sabines attacked Rome sometime near the beginning of Romulus's reign in the eighth century B.C. (in retaliation for the Roman abduction of the Sabine women). A young woman named Tarpeia, daughter of Spurius Tarpeius, leader of Rome's central fortress, supposedly played a key role in the episode. When the Sabine king, Titus Tatius, and his men approached the fortress, Tarpeia secretly arranged a meeting between herself and Tatius. What happened next is disputed, for two conflicting versions of the story have survived. In the first, the young woman gave Tatius the keys to the fortress in exchange for the gold bracelets and rings of his men, in which case she was a traitor to Rome. In the other, more popular story, Tarpeia gave Tatius the keys intending to trick him. In exchange for them, the Sabine soldiers gave her their shields; and without them, these men were unable to defend themselves properly against a counterattack led by Romulus. In this second story, therefore, Tarpeia was a hero who saved the city. In any case, the hill on which the fortress sat was called the Tarpeian Hill, after her. (Later, it came to be known as the Capitoline Hill.)

threatened their own vastly different culture, rigorous country life, and puritanical ideals. Rome herself [came to look] like an Etruscan city. For centuries after the Etruscan monarchy, the art of Rome was still nearly all Etruscan.[11]

Just as the wealth and finery of the Etruscan nobles clashed with the relative austerity of Roman life at all social levels, so too did the status and treatment of Etruscan women. Abundant archaeological evidence shows that Etruscan women (at least those in the upper classes, since most of the evidence is about them) were socially emancipated. Tomb sculptures and paintings show women dining, attending sporting contests, and sharing in other activities equally with men. This and other evidence suggest that Etruscan women enjoyed much higher social status than Roman women.

Roman Disdain for Etruscan Women

Etruscan women most certainly were more liberated than the Greek women who inhabited the region southeast of Rome. Although the treatment of women varied somewhat from one Greek area to another, in general Greek women were even more socially subservient and marginalized than Roman women. The average Greek woman spent most of her time at home, was not allowed to attend dinner parties given by her husband, and had to retire to the "women's quarters" in the back of the house when men from outside the family were visiting.

It is not surprising, then, that both Greek and Roman male observers were highly critical of Etruscan women, whose lives they saw as much too free and permissive. The fourth-century Greek historian Theopompus was typical in perpetuating a biased and distorted view of so-called Etruscan decadence:

> It is normal for the Etruscans to share their women in common. These women take great care of their bodies and exercise bare, exposing their bodies even before men and among themselves, for it is not shameful for them to appear almost naked. . . . The Etruscans raise all the children that are born, not knowing who the father is of each one. The children eventually live like those who brought them up, and have many drinking parties, and they too make love with all the women. [12]

There is no evidence for such promiscuous behavior by Etruscan women outside of some highly prejudiced Greek and Roman accounts. But the very fact that educated Roman men disapproved so much of Etruscan women may explain, at least in part, changes in the way they came to treat their own women. Many experts on Roman law contend that, very early in Rome's history, women had inheritance rights similar to men's, but by the early Republic women had lost most of these rights. If this is true, it is highly plausible that Roman women first gained these rights through the enlightened influence of the Etruscans. Then, in establishing the Republic, the Romans threw out their Etruscan-born king and his courtiers. This act may well have been accompanied by a general negative reaction to overt Etruscan ideas and customs, all to emphasize that Rome was not and never had been an Etruscan city. A tightening of male control over Roman women could have been part of this reaction.

In the Framework of the Family

It stands to reason, then, that the status, rights, and privileges of Roman women in early republican times were much closer to those of Greek women than those of Etruscan women (though Roman women were not quite as restricted as Greek women). Both as members of the community and as individuals, Greek and Roman women existed first and foremost within the traditional framework of the family. Even later, in Livy's day and on into the Empire, the Roman family (*familia,* or "household") remained the most basic and time-honored social unit. Most Roman families appear to have been nuclear, consisting of father, mother, and their children and slaves (although a few families were extended to include grandparents, uncles, aunts, cousins, and/or in-laws).

The head of the family was the paterfamilias, usually the oldest father present. By ancient tradition, he held power and authority known as *patria potestas* over all other members of the household, including his daughters. This power gave him the right to control all property earned or acquired by these dependents, to regulate and punish them, and even to decide whether a newborn infant should be reared or exposed (left outside to die).

These, at least, were the powers that early custom and law allowed the paterfamilias. In actual practice, most family heads were not merciless tyrants, and cases of fathers throwing their wives or children out or killing them were relatively rare, even in Rome's earlier centuries. Over time, new laws set certain restrictions on the *patria potestas,* and in any case, calls from a father's relatives, friends, and peers for him to act reasonably tended to restrain him from unusually cruel behavior. According to custom, he was obliged to convene a council of relatives and friends when he was considering punishing his children severely, and in such cases he usually abided by the council's verdict.

By tradition, the materfamilias, the paterfamilias's wife or mother, was also

Patriotic Women Donate Their Jewelry

O ne of the many examples from Roman legend describing patriotic behavior by Roman women concerns the reaction to a force of invading Gauls (tribesmen from central Europe) who seized control of Rome in 390 B.C. The Romans endeavored to bribe the Gauls to leave, and according to Livy in his Roman history:

When it was found that there was not enough gold in the treasury to

pay the Gauls the agreed sum, contributions from the [city's] women [were] accepted, to avoid touching what was consecrated [i.e., golden offerings in the temples of the gods]. The women who had contributed were formally thanked, and were further granted the privilege, hitherto [before this] confined to men, of having laudatory orations pronounced at their funerals.

A Roman man and his wife are depicted in this second-century A.D. *funerary monument.*

subject to the absolute authority of the male head of household. Though early Roman women were considered citizens, like women in other ancient societies, they did not enjoy the same rights and social prominence as male citizens. An exception was in the area of religion. Although women in Rome could not vote or hold public office at any time in Rome's long history, even in the Monarchy and early Republic they could become public priestesses, who were highly respected.

According to later Roman writers, male treatment of women as inferiors in the early years of the Republic was the result of men's belief that they were more intelligent and competent than women. As Cicero described it, "Our ancestors estab-

lished the rule that all women, because of their weakness of intellect, should be under the power of guardians." [13] These guardians, or tutors, were always men, who controlled the property of women and barred them from initiating divorce, making wills, and other legal procedures. "The tutor as a rule was a relative," University of Parma scholar Eva Cantarella explains,

but sometimes a person was designated by the father's will or designated by a magistrate. The reason for this discrimination (at least in the first centuries of the city's history) was clear: [in the opinion of men] women were not able to take care of themselves. . . . It is no exaggeration to say that guardianship for life effectively nullified the legal capacities of Roman women. They could dispose of their acknowledged rights only with the mediation and assent of a man. [14]

Luckily for Roman women, by Cicero's time society had become somewhat more enlightened and less chauvinistic about the so-called gentler sex. His writings and those of other first-century-B.C. Roman men reveal a certain relaxation of traditional, strict male control of women. It would be an exaggeration to call it *emancipation* in the modern sense of the word. But the lot of at least some Roman women had improved measurably since the early Republic, a trend that would continue in the years to come.

Women of Ancient Rome

Chapter 2:
Upper-Class Women Gain Rights and Autonomy

By the second and first centuries B.C., the lot of Roman women had improved considerably, and it continued to improve in the first two centuries of the Empire. Though they still had no political rights, many women gained the right to file for divorce at will and to inherit and control their own property, and a few came to administer quite sizable fortunes.

Moreover, evidence shows that in at least some Roman households, wives became more men's partners than their legal charges and servants. Some women regularly attended parties and public functions with their husbands and enjoyed a degree of personal freedom unprecedented in the ancient world. The high degree of love and respect that some men came to feel for their wives is illustrated in a letter penned by Pliny the Younger to his wife, Calpurnia, while she was away:

> You cannot believe how much I miss you. I love you so much, and we are not used to separations. So I stay awake most of the night thinking of you, and by day I find my feet carry-ing me . . . to your room at the times I usually visited you; then finding it empty I depart, as sick and sorrowful as a lover locked out. [15]

It is important to point out that Calpurnia was an upper-class Roman woman, as were those who owned and administered estates and fortunes. The privileges and benefits of being born into families with wealth and high social rank also allowed a few women to acquire some real, though usually indirect, political power. The wives, mothers, and daughters of army officers and politicians, even emperors, variously groomed and molded their sons for high office; pestered, cajoled, offered advice to, or otherwise influenced their husbands behind the scenes; and took part in dangerous schemes and conspiracies to advance their own, their sons', or their families' interests. These are the Roman women we know most about, since the bulk of the surviving written evidence describes them rather than poorer women.

By the second century B.C., many Roman women could read and write.

Economic Factors Aid Women

The process by which upper-class women gained better treatment and more respect and autonomy in Rome was gradual and most often involved economic factors. One early major turning point occurred during the Second Punic War (218–201 B.C.), a huge and devastating conflict in which Rome fought and defeated the empire of Carthage (centered in North Africa). In 215 B.C., at the height of the war, the Roman government, which badly needed money to support the army, placed a stiff tax on well-to-do independent women. Rome also passed the Lex Oppia, an aus-terity law that forbade women from indulging in various luxuries. (Among the restrictions were that each woman was limited to a half-ounce of gold and no women could ride in carriages within a mile of the capital city.) Out of a sense of patriotism, women lived with such imposi-tions during the course of the war. But when the conflict ended and the law remained in force, they balked. In 195 B.C. thousands of women angrily demonstrated in the streets, and anx-ious Roman leaders backed down and repealed the Oppian law.

Probably only a few of these demon-strating women were wealthy or came from rich families. But the number of such women began to increase signifi-cantly in the following years. Immediately after its victory over Carthage, Rome commenced the conquest of the Greek lands of the eastern Mediterranean; and large numbers of military commanders and other Roman men became rich (or rich ones got richer) from plunder and business ventures. This placed increased wealth, via dowries and inheritances, in the hands of the female relatives of such men. That so many women were becom-ing rich so fast bothered many legislators, who in 169 B.C. attempted to limit the trend by passing the Lex Voconia, which forbade a wealthy man from leaving a daughter more than half his fortune in his will.

Nevertheless, the trend continued. The combination of access to wealth and the frequent absence of husbands, who were away fighting in wars, helped to increase the wealth and personal autonomy of many upper-class married women. Elaine Fantham writes,

> While the military commander was away campaigning for years at a time in Macedonia or Spain his wife would have a household staff to help her manage his affairs; admittedly the law still required women to conduct any legal business through the intermediary of a male tutor, but it became increasingly common for women to appoint their own puppets, freedmen [freed slaves], or family clients who would do what they were told. [16]

Such autonomy continued to increase in the century that followed, partly for the same reasons. In the first century B.C., the Republic was shaken to its foundation by a series of devastating civil wars and political purges that killed tens of thousands of Roman men, many of them well-to-do. This left many women either temporarily or permanently in charge of households or free to seek other, perhaps more successful, husbands. "These generations had seen the social order itself repeatedly disrupted," says Fantham.

Women were released from surveillance by the absence of their menfolk on campaign, in overseas administration, or during the civil war in flight or exile. While older or more sober women showed their emancipation by taking on responsibility for family finances, political negotiations, or petitions for their husbands' survival, others in less stable marriages might see no reason for fidelity, and daughters married off as a political bond between their father and his allies (or even former enemies) might assert themselves. [17]

A fanciful medieval painting depicts Roman women protesting the Oppian law.

These developments explain how several decades later (ca. A.D. 65) a Pompeiian woman was both independent and wealthy enough to post the following ad on a local wall:

On the estate of Julia Felix, the daughter of Spurius Felix, the following are for rent: an elegant bath suitable for the best people, shops, rooms above them, and second story apartments, from the Ides of August [August 15] until the Ides of August five years hence, after which the lease may be renewed by simple agreement.[18]

Educating Young Women

Another factor that helped improve the social position and personal autonomy of

Cornelia's Jewels

Few Roman women were more fondly remembered than Cornelia, who lived in the second century B.C. The second daughter of the renowned general Scipio Africanus and mother of two noted social reformers, the Gracchi brothers (Gaius and Tiberius), she became a model for the ideal, virtuous Roman matron. After the death of her husband, Sempronius Gracchus, in 153 B.C., Cornelia managed the estate and educated their twelve children with such skill and fortitude that she remained a strong influence on all of them throughout their lives. According to the Greek biographer Plutarch, when someone asked to see her valuable gems, she summoned her sons and declared them to be her jewels.

Cornelia embraces her "jewels"—her sons, Gaius and Tiberius.

upper-class women was their education. They were better educated than lower-class women (as well as many lower-class men). And reading and writing skills increased their chances of success in managing money, estates, business affairs, and political intrigues.

Very few young women, rich or poor, received any significant schooling in the less enlightened days of the early Republic. From the third century B.C. on, however, educational opportunities for both girls and boys increased. Young people age seven to eleven from families who could afford it went to a *ludus,* a private elementary school, which was supported by their parents rather than the state.[19] At a typical elementary school, which consisted of a single rented room, often in the rear of a shop, the teacher (*magister* or *litterator*) taught basic Latin reading and writing skills, and also some simple arithmetic, to about twelve students at a time.

At about the age of eleven, girls usually left school. Some continued their education at home, receiving instruction from their parents or private tutors (in this case teachers, not guardians). Although most of these young women began preparing for marriage, which usually occurred when they were about fourteen or fifteen, some continued their home studies with their tutors or new husbands (who were almost always several years older than their brides).

Probably some of the fathers who educated their daughters in this manner did so

Many Roman girls were tutored at home in reading, writing, and numbers.

because they thought it would better the young women's chances of attracting suitable high-placed husbands. But other fathers came to believe that educating women was also the fair and ethical thing to do. The noted first-century-A.D. philosopher and teacher Musonius Rufus offered the following rationale, which at least some Roman men accepted:

Women have received from the gods the same ability to reason that men have. We men employ reasoning in our relations with others and so far as possible in everything we do, whether it is good or bad, or noble or shameful. Likewise women have the same senses as men, sight, hearing, smell, and all the rest.... In addition, it is not men

Loyal and Feisty Fulvia

F ulvia, the first wife of the powerful general Mark Antony, played a prominent part in the power struggles following the assassination of Antony's mentor, Julius Caesar, in the 40s B.C. When Antony was away from Rome, Fulvia acted as one of his principal agents in the capital and worked diligently to promote his interests. Eventually, she came to blows with Caesar's adopted son, Octavian, whom she rightly viewed as a political threat to Antony's future. After Fulvia and Antony's brother, Lucius, launched a failed military campaign against Octavian in 41 B.C., they fled to Athens. There, the loyal and feisty woman met with Antony, who surprised her by sternly condemning her feud with Octavian. Crushed, she died soon afterward.

alone who possess eagerness and a natural inclination towards virtue, but women also. Women are pleased no less than men by noble and just deeds, and reject the opposite of such actions. . . . It is reasonable, then, for me to think that women ought to be educated similarly to men in respect of virtue, and they must be taught starting when they are children. . . . From these lessons reasoning is developed in both girls and boys, and there is no distinction between them. . . . [After being taught what one should do and not do in life] both men and women will inevitably be sensible.[20]

The Uses of Learning and Talent

Musonius Rufus was mistaken in thinking that educating either men or women would ensure more virtuous behavior. As is true of both sexes in any age, upper-class Roman women could end up squandering their educations and other benefits of their privileged upbringings. An example was recorded by the first-century-B.C. Roman historian Sallust in his book about the conspiracy of Catiline, which occurred in 63 B.C. A disgruntled aristocrat, Catiline planned to kill Cicero and the other consul (chief government administrator) and seize control of the state. Among those accused of joining the plot was Sempronia, a well-to-do matron who supposedly allowed the leading conspirators to meet in her house. Sallust vigorously denounced her as an indecent and willful woman, yet he also pointed out her intelligence, fine education, and good breeding, which he felt she had wasted:

Fortune had favored her abundantly, not only with birth and beauty, but with a good husband and children. Well educated in Greek and Latin literature, she had greater skill in lyre-playing and dancing than there is any need for a respectable woman to acquire, besides many other accomplishments. . . . Her abilities were not to be despised. She could write poetry, crack a joke, and converse at will with decorum, tender feeling, or wantonness; she was in fact a woman of ready wit and considerable charm.[21]

Unlike Sempronia (assuming she was guilty, which is uncertain), most educated women put their learning to good use, even if it was only to correspond with other educated women in polite society. Recent excavations of a Roman fort at Vindolanda, in northern Britain, have revealed more than fifteen hundred documents (many consisting of thin wooden sheets, called leaf tablets, inscribed with ink). Some were written by and to women. In one, Claudia Severa, the wife of the commander of a neighboring fort, writes to Sulpicia Lepidina, the wife of Vindolanda's commander, Flavius Cerialis:

Greetings. I send you a warm invitation to come to us on September 11th, for my birthday celebrations, to make my day more enjoyable by your presence. Give my greetings to your Cerialis. My [husband] Aelius greets you and your sons. I will expect you sister. Farewell sister, my dearest soul, as I hope to prosper, and greetings.[22]

A few women went further and used their writing skills to produce works of prose and poetry, no small feat in a literary world completely dominated by men. Sallust mentioned Sempronia's ability as a poetess, for example. In his *Annals,* Tacitus cites as one of his references an autobiography by Agrippina the Younger, mother of the emperor Nero: "This incident . . . I found in the memoirs of the daughter of Agrippina [the Elder] . . . in which she recorded for posterity her life and her family's fortunes."[23] Agrippina's book, unfortunately now lost, must have been of sufficient detail and quality for one of the greatest ancient historians to feel confident in using it as reference material.

The only Roman woman writer whose works have survived in more than a few fragments was Sulpicia, who lived in the first century B.C. She was a ward of M. Valerius Messala Corvinus, a wealthy arts patron who subsidized a circle of poets, including Albius Tibullus. Tibullus befriended Sulpicia, and her poems have survived in the form of quotations within his own works. In this sample, she tells how it is better to quash gossip mongers by openly admitting her secret love affair:

Agrippina the Elder

T he granddaughter of Augustus, the first emperor, Agrippina the Elder (ca. 14 B.C.–A.D. 33) is best known for her avid dislike for the second emperor, Tiberius. Agrippina married the talented and popular general Germanicus, Tiberius's nephew, and had nine children by him, including the third emperor, Caligula. Devoted to her husband, she joined him on his campaigns in Germany and showed both courage and generosity by personally distributing food and clothing to the soldiers during a time of crisis. Along with Germanicus, she held dear Rome's old republican ideals, which put them on a collision course with Tiberius and his henchman, Sejanus. When the emperor ordered Germanicus to a post in faraway Syria, Agrippina followed her husband, and after he died under mysterious circumstances, she became convinced that Tiberius had arranged the murder. She then became openly hostile to the emperor, who finally exiled her. Soon after, she starved herself to death at the age of forty-seven.

This painting by the eighteenth-century British artist Benjamin West shows Agrippina the Elder arriving in Italy with the ashes of her husband, Germanicus.

At last a love had come of such a kind that my shame, Gossip, would be greater if I kept it covered than if I laid it bare. Cythera, implored by my verses, brought that man to me and gave him into my embrace. Venus [goddess of love] kept her promise; let anyone talk about my joy who—it's said—never had any of his own. I would not want to send anything to him on sealed tablets, lest anyone should read it before my own love does; but my sin is a joy, though it's tiresome to keep a straight face for gossip's sake. Let it be said that I was a worthy woman, with a worthy man.[24]

The popular first-century-A.D. humorist Martial mentions another poetess named Sulpicia, who flourished about a century after the first one. "She teaches chaste and honest loves," he says, "the games, the delights, the humor of love. He who appreciates her poetry will say that no woman was more mischievous, and no woman more modest."[25]

Models of Old-Fashioned Virtue

Even though in the society that nurtured the two Sulpicias women had more economic clout, visibility, and voice than in past ages, they were still largely dominated by men. And many, if not most, men continued to marginalize and stereotype

A bust of the philosopher Seneca, who praised his mother in a long letter.

women as they had in the past. The Roman matron, especially one who inhabited polite, upper-class circles, still symbolized old-fashioned virtues, as exemplified in the stories of Veturia, Lucretia, and other legendary heroines. Male writers often viewed and measured the women of their own day in these terms. In the A.D. 40s, while in exile (after being accused of having an affair with an emperor's sister), the philosopher Seneca wrote a long letter to cheer up his despondent mother. In this excerpt, he praises her for holding fast to old-fashioned Roman values such as austerity and modesty:

Unchastity, the greatest plague of our age, has but the majority of womankind in a different category from yours; gems nor pearls have tempted you; its glitter has not persuaded you that wealth is man's greatest good. You were well brought up in an old-fashioned and strict household, and you have never been led astray by the imitation of worse women, which is a hazard even to good ones. You have never been ashamed of your children, as though their number taunted you with your years; you have never concealed your pregnancy as an unsightly parcel, as do other women whose sole claim for approval is their beauty. . . . You have not defiled your face with paint and . . . cosmetics; you never fancied sheer dresses that revealed as much on as off. Your unique jewel, your fairest beauty, which time cannot wither, your greatest glory, is your proven modesty. You cannot, therefore, hold your sex up as a justification for your grief, for your virtues set you apart from your sex. You must be as superior to a woman's tears as you are to her vices. [26]

Young women, too, could be seen as models of female virtue, obedience, restraint, and propriety, as revealed by Pliny the Younger in this touching letter lamenting the death of the daughter of a well-to-do friend:

I am writing to you in great distress. Our friend Fundanus has lost his younger daughter. I never saw a girl so gay and lovable, so deserving of a longer life or even a life to last forever. She had not yet reached the age of fourteen, and yet she combined the wisdom of age and dignity of womanhood with the sweetness and modesty of youth and innocence. She would cling to her father's neck, and embrace us, his friends, with

A bust of Livia, wife of Augustus and first empress of Rome.

Women of Ancient Rome

The Infamous Younger Agrippina

grippina the Younger (A.D. 15–59) was the daughter of a Roman general, Germanicus, and Agrippina the Elder, as well as the mother of the notorious emperor Nero. In the year 28, the younger Agrippina married an unsavory nobleman, Gnaeus Domitius Ahenobarbus, and nine years later gave birth to Nero, whom she thereafter schemed to put on the throne. When her husband died in 39, the reigning emperor, Caligula, suspected her of plotting against him and exiled her. But his successor, Claudius, her uncle, recalled her in 41 and in 49 married her. Soon she became unusually influential in the royal bureaucracy, even assuming a role in distributing funds. In 54, Agrippina apparently poisoned Claudius and fulfilled her dream of making her son emperor. Because Nero was only seventeen when he ascended the throne, she practically ran the Empire single-handedly during the early years of his reign. Eventually, though, he grew tired and jealous of her and began plotting her death. After a failed plot to drown her by rigging her ship to sink, Nero sent some soldiers to stab her to death. Supposedly, she challenged them to strike first in her abdomen, in which she had carried her ungrateful son, and they did so.

modest affection; she loved her nurses, her attendants and her teachers, each one for the service given her; she applied herself intelligently to her books and was moderate and restrained in her play. She bore her illness with patient resignation and, indeed, with courage; she obeyed her doctors' orders, cheered her sister and father, and by sheer force of will carried on after her physical strength had failed her. This will power remained with her to the end, and neither the length of her illness nor fear of death could break it. So she has left us all the more sad reason for lamenting our loss. Hers is a truly tragic and untimely end. Death itself was not so cruel as the moment of its coming. [27]

Livia, Augusta of Rome

Of course, not all upper-class women were content to be obedient and occupy polite social niches men found socially acceptable. The pages of Tacitus, Suetonius, and other ancient historians reveal in some detail the exploits of a handful of truly ambitious and powerful women in imperial times. Usually, they attained their influence and authority

The Notorious Messalina

Valeria Messalina, the third wife of the emperor Claudius, was empress of Rome from 41 to 48. One of the most notorious women in history, she became known for her political intrigues and sexual and other excesses. Dominating court life, she influenced many of her husband's decisions, all the while silencing her political opponents and going through a veritable stable of lovers behind her husband's back. Thanks to a powerful courtier, Narcissus, Claudius eventually found out and assented to Messalina's execution. The shaken, saddened emperor vowed never to marry again, but he did so the following year, to another schemer—Agrippina the Younger.

Messalina, Claudius's third wife, was famous for her numerous sexual partners.

partly by circumstance (being born into the right family at the right time) and partly through personal talent and sheer strength of purpose and action.

Livia, the wife of the first emperor, Augustus, set the precedent that a number of other ambitious noblewomen would later follow. In his will, Augustus left his wife a third of his estate; he left the remainder to her son, Tiberius (from a previous marriage and therefore Augustus's adoptive son), who became the second emperor. The will also stipulated that she should receive the title of Augusta, or "mother of the emperor." This gave her an honorific role in public life, something no other women enjoyed (with the exception of a handful of priestesses). Livia also received other honors, including the right to sit with high priestesses in the theater, immunity from the wealth restrictions of the Lex Voconia, and the striking of coins bearing her image. The Senate even debated whether to bestow on her the title of *parens patriae* ("parent of the country").

Tiberius stepped in and vetoed this senatorial honor, however. He worried, probably rightly, that his mother might acquire enough power and prestige to become literally coruler with him, thus diminishing his own powerful position. It did not help that the title Augusta could be interpreted to mean "empress" as much as queen mother. So the new emperor began to avoid Livia and did everything he could to keep her from amassing any more authority and prestige. He even nullified her will after her death.

Had Tiberius given his mother freer rein, her deeds may well have proven to skeptical Romans that an intelligent woman did have the ability to hold and execute a major political office, and in time this may have greatly accelerated the pace of women's emancipation in the Empire. But this never happened. In the centuries to come, the Augustas and other palace noblewomen—some of them kind and reputable, others cruel and corrupt—struggled to assert themselves in whatever way they could in the imperial court.

The Three Ambitious Julias

Perhaps none of these powerful women were more remarkable than Julia Domna and her sister and niece, who manipulated and eventually dominated imperial politics in the first three decades of the third century. The second wife of the emperor Septimius Severus, Julia Domna was empress of Rome from 193 to 211. She was noted for her intelligence and interest in the arts and philosophy and is said to have invited numerous intellectuals to the court. After her husband died in 211, the next emperor, her son Caracalla, put her in charge of imperial correspondence and petitions and often followed her political advice.

After Caracalla and Julia Domna died, her sister Julia Maesa organized a plot to destroy the new ruler, Macrinus, and make her grandson Elagabalus emperor.

This bust of Julia Domna captures her unusual intelligence and strong will.

The conspiracy succeeded. Julia Maesa completely dominated the young man, practically ruling the Empire in his stead, after which she next groomed her other grandson, Severus Alexander, for the throne. When the latter became emperor after Elagabalus's murder in 222, she played a prominent role in his administration, influencing many of his decisions.

As for Julia Mamaea, Severus Alexander's mother, at first her influence was limited by her mother's commanding presence. But when Julia Maesa died in 226, Julia Mamaea stepped forward to become nothing less than the Empire's virtual ruler, overseeing most of her son's activities and influencing his decisions. According to ancient accounts, she was so domineering and greedy for power and wealth that she eventually made the mistake of alienating the military. A group of soldiers eventually assassinated her and her son, ending the so-called Severan dynasty of rulers.

Whether the overweening ambition and scheming of the three Julias hurt the chances for other upper-class women to succeed in the political arena is debatable. What is certain is that never again in Rome's history did a group of women in one family wield so much power. A few individual women later exerted various degrees of influence over emperors and generals. But for the most part Roman politics remained a male sphere.

Chapter 3:
Social Status and Occupations of Lower-Class Women

Much less is known about lower-class Roman women and their lives than about upper-class ones. This is partly because most women did not write about themselves (and the works of those few who did have not survived). Also, male writers only rarely mentioned lower-class women in their writings. "It must be evident that lower-class women were always more numerous," Sarah Pomeroy remarks, "but less notorious—the activities of celebrities tend to captivate the historical imagination."[28]

Therefore, most of the inadequate evidence regarding the lives of lower-class women comes from scattered references to the rights and duties of slaves and freedwomen in laws and legal opinions. It also comes from inscriptions, including graffiti on buildings and tomb epitaphs. Such epitaphs often include not only the woman's name but also several of the following: her status (slave, freedwoman, or freeborn woman); the name of her owner or former owner; her husband's name; the length of their marriage and her age at death; the number of their children, if any; her occupation or work specialty; and sometimes information about her looks and character. Consider the following example, composed in the first century B.C. (The words in quotes are not those of the deceased; it was common custom for an epitaph writer to make it seem as if the dead person was speaking for him- or herself.)

[The tomb] of Eucharis, freedwoman of Licinia, an unmarried girl who was educated and learned in every skill. She lived 14 years. Ah, as you look with wandering eye at the house of death, stay your foot and read what is inscribed here. This is what a father's love gave his daughter, where the remains of her body lie gathered. . . . "I was educated and taught as if by the hands of the Muses [goddesses of the arts]. I adorned the nobility's festivals with my dancing, and first appeared before the common people in a Greek play. But now here in this tomb my enemies the Fates have

This first-century A.D. Roman funerary monument shows a butcher, L. Aurelius Hermia, bidding farewell to his devoted wife, Aurelia Philematio.

placed my body's ashes. The patrons of learning—devotion, passion, praise, honor—are silenced by my burnt corpse and by my death. His child, I left lamentation to my father, though born after him, I precede him in the day of my death. Now I observe my fourteenth birthday here among the shadows in Death's ageless home. I beg you when you leave, ask that the earth lie light upon me."[29]

From this inscription we learn that Eucharis began as the slave of a woman named Licinia, who freed her sometime before she turned fourteen; that the girl was unmarried; that she was well educated, probably in Licinia's household; that Eucharis made a living as an actress; and that her body was cremated. That her father, presumably a working-class freedman, loved her deeply pervades the entire message. In a similar manner, modern scholars attempt to piece together a picture, however incomplete, of the status, rights (or lack thereof), duties, occupations, and working conditions of Rome's female slaves, freedwomen, and poorer freeborn women.

Female Household Slaves

Of all Roman women, those who were slaves had the lowest social status and fewest rights. Historians estimate that by the reign of Augustus, at the start of the Empire, fully one-third of Italy's population (which may have been about 7 million people) were slaves. So about a third of Roman women in Italy may have been slaves (assuming there were roughly equal numbers of male and female slaves, which is not certain). Not only were slaves numerous, but slavery was a very complex institution in Rome; slaves and freedmen, along with masters and former masters, pervaded all niches of society. And a female slave was trapped within a tangled web of entrenched laws, customs, and practices, most of which were designed to benefit her master and other freeborn Romans rather than herself.

On the plus side, some slaves lived in more comfortable surroundings and received better treatment than others. Most of those who worked in households in cities and towns, for example, enjoyed more privileges and comforts than those who labored on farms and in mines. In particular, *vernae,* those slaves born and reared in the household, were often treated with

A well-to-do Roman matron is attended by her slaves. Slaves who worked in wealthy households had more comfortable lives than those who worked on farms.

nearly as much care and affection as the master's own children. As historian L.P. Wilkinson says, "Normal masters could hardly fail, even if half-ashamedly, to have a soft spot for characters they had seen toddling and growing up about the place."[30] Also, in the elegant surroundings of more well-to-do households, especially those of kind masters, slaves often ate and dressed better and were safer and more secure than most poor free Romans.

There were many more negatives than pluses, however, for a female household slave. First, like all Roman slaves, she had little or no control over her own life and fate. She was expected first and foremost to obey her master, to do whatever work he assigned without complaint, to go and come only as he allowed, and to satisfy his every whim, no matter how demanding, odd, or degrading. The absolute power of a master over a slave was actually an extension of the authority held by the paterfamilias over the free members of his family. This power gave the master the right to control the slave's entire life and to punish her at his own will and discretion. Thus, in the eyes of the law she was no different than a sheep, a horse, or any other animal exploited by an owner. Just as an owner might beat a horse to get it to perform better, he might flog or otherwise abuse a female slave who did not satisfactorily perform her duties.

These duties were mainly those seen as "women's work" in virtually all ancient societies: cleaning, spinning and weaving, making clothes, preparing food and cooking, helping to deliver babies, and taking care of children. In Rome, supplying the male master with sex on demand was also frequently a duty of a female slave. Today, such exploitation of a person's servile position is seen as a serious form of abuse, but throughout most of their history, the Romans, both masters and slaves, accepted it as a natural occurrence, something expected of a slave. Even the second-century-B.C. statesman Cato the Elder, a staunch proponent of old-fashioned morality, indulged in the practice. Plutarch wrote that after Cato's wife died, "He consoled himself with a young slave girl, who came to his room secretly to sleep with him. This intrigue soon came to light, as might be expected in a small household."[31] Furthermore, it was quite common in such situations for the master's wife to look the other way or even openly accept such behavior.

The Lot of Farm Slaves

Female farm slaves suffered this same sort of abuse in addition to other hardships. Their lives were generally harsher, with relentless physical labor that made them age and die quicker than most other young women. In his treatise on agriculture, the first-century-B.C. Roman scholar Marcus

Spinning Yarn and Weaving Cloth

Spinning and weaving were among the principal duties of lower-class Roman women. The main tools they used were the spindle and distaff. The spindle was a wooden or bone rod about eight inches long that was slightly thicker toward the lower end; attached to it was a whorl, a small weight that acted like a flywheel to keep it spinning. The distaff was a forked stick that held a bundle of fibers. The spinner pulled a few fibers out of the distaff, twisted them together with her fingers, and then tied them to the spindle. Grasping the distaff with her left hand, she allowed the spindle to hang and with her right hand set it spinning. As she pulled more fibers from the distaff, the rotating spindle twisted them into a thread of yarn.

Once a sufficient amount of yarn had been spun, it was time to begin weaving it. The most common loom in use in the Roman world consisted of two vertical pieces of wood connected at the top by a horizontal beam. The weaver hung a row of vertical threads (the warp) from the beam and weighted them at the bottom using stone or baked clay loom weights. Using a rod (heddle), she moved the odd-numbered warp threads backward and forward, working in horizontal threads (the weft) through a gap in the frame. The warp and weft threads thus intertwined to produce the cloth.

These drawings based on ancient sculptures show Roman women operating looms. Almost all women were expected to engage in spinning and weaving.

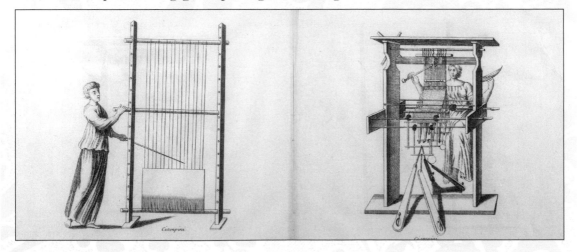

Terentius Varro described the lot of such unfortunate individuals:

> In the case of those who tend the herds in mountain valleys and wooded lands and keep off the rains . . . by makeshift huts, many have thought it advisable to send along women to follow the herds, prepare food for the herdsmen, and make them more diligent. Such women should, however, be strong and not ill-looking. In many places they are not inferior to the men at work . . . being able either to tend the herd or carry firewood and cook the food, or to keep things in order in their huts. As to feeding their young, I merely remark that in most cases they suckle them as well as bear them. . . . Mothers [often carry] logs and children at the breast at the same time, sometimes one, sometimes two. . . . It often happens that a pregnant woman, when her time has come,

A group of agricultural slaves deemed dangerous enough to lock up at the end of their day's work receive their evening allotment of bread.

Women of Ancient Rome

A Slave Woman Ends Up Rich

Musa was not the only Roman slave woman who hobnobbed with the wealthy and famous and managed to carve out a comfortable life for herself. Acte, a palace slave, had been freed by the emperor Claudius (reigned A.D. 41–54). She eventually caught the eye of Claudius's successor, the young Nero, and they became lovers in the second year of his reign (A.D. 55). The two tried to keep the relationship a secret from Nero's powerful, overbearing mother, Agrippina the Younger, who did not want him wasting his time with "riffraff." But Agrippina found out and denounced Acte. This only made Nero want the young girl more, and his mother finally saw that her best strategy was to pretend to accept the romance while scheming against the lovers behind their backs.

Fearing for her life, Acte told Nero about some nasty rumors claiming that Agrippina and her son were committing incest together; for this and other reasons, in A.D. 59 the emperor had his mother killed. By this time, Nero had grown tired of Acte. But fortunately for her, he had given her some estates as gifts, so she lived a comfortable life. When the Roman people turned against Nero and he committed suicide a few years later, Acte proved that she had really loved him. She volunteered to dress his body in white robes and carry his ashes to his tomb, and she paid two thousand gold pieces toward the expenses for his funeral.

steps aside a little way out of her work, bears her child there, and brings it back so soon that you would say she had not borne it but found it. [32]

Slightly better was the situation of a female companion of a male slave who managed a farm for the owner. The manager was called a *vilicus*, she a *vilica*. Her function was apparently twofold—to keep the manager satisfied and happy, and therefore more apt to discharge his duties faithfully, and to aid him in those duties. A first-century-A.D. estate owner, Lucius Junius Columella, who wrote a book on farm management, describes her not only as a laborer, expected to do spinning, weaving, and other traditional women's work, but also as a nurse in charge of a small on-site hospital. "What she must continually be careful about," he states,

is to go round once the slaves have left the farmhouse and look for anyone who ought to be out working in the fields; and if she finds any malingerer

A Dutiful Wife Remembered

This epitaph for a dead freedwoman, dating from the first century B.C. (and quoted in Jo-Ann Shelton's *As the Romans Did*), was composed by her husband. Relationships like the one described, between young girls and grown men, were not unusual. It is possible that he bought her as his slave when he himself was still a slave and that they were freed together.

"I was called, while alive, Aurelia Philematium, a woman chaste and modest, unsoiled by the common crowd, faithful to her husband. My husband, whom alas, I now left, was a fellow freedman. He was truly like a father to me. When I was seven years old he embraced me [i.e., became her master, lover, or both]. Now I am forty and in the power of death. Through my constant care, my husband flourished."

Portraits of a man and wife on their second-century A.D. funerary stele. Many surviving tomb epitaphs describe love between husbands and wives.

inside, who has escaped the notice of her husband . . . she must ask why he is not at work and find out whether he has stayed behind because he feels ill or because he is lazy. If she finds that this is the case, she must immediately take him to the sickroom, even if he is only pretending to be ill. . . . She should occasionally go and open up the sickroom even if there aren't any patients there, and clean it so that it is in an orderly and healthy state to receive anyone who may fall ill. [33]

Slave Marriages

The reason why a *vilica* must be called a "female companion" rather than a wife is that she and the man she lived with could not marry, at least not formally; the law did not recognize the union between two slaves. However, masters usually allowed slaves to engage in an informal marital arrangement called *contubernium*, or "cohabitation." Although such a union was not legally valid and any children it produced were illegitimate, the slaves involved took it seriously and thought of each other as husband and wife. Sarah Pomeroy explains why it was in a master's interest to allow such unions:

It improved morale and produced slave children who were the master's to keep in his household or to dispose of as he wished. Slaves tended to marry other slaves, and were likely to marry within their master's *familia.* With permission, a slave might marry a slave from another *familia* or a free person. However, if a male slave married a female outside his master's *familia,* the master lost the profit that might be gained from the offspring, since the children belonged to the mother if she were free, or to her master if she was a slave. Hence such a marriage might not be permitted. [34]

Manumission

Indeed, the issue of children was important to female slaves as well as masters. Many, if not most, enslaved women must have dreamed of manumission (gaining freedom), if for no other reason than to ensure that their children would be free and legitimate. There were a number of ways by which a female slave could be manumitted and acquire the status of freedwoman. If she had borne the master children, for instance, his freeing and marrying her made these children legitimate. (By contrast, society frowned on freeborn women freeing and marrying male slaves; and a law passed in the early third century A.D. forbade the practice.)

Aside from improving her children's lot in life, usually the acquisition of freedom brought such a woman little more than a small upgrade in legal and social status. In at least one case, though, circumstances allowed an Italian slave woman to become the ruler of a realm (though not the Roman one). Her name was Musa. As Marjorie and Benjamin Lightman tell it,

In 20 B.C. Musa was part of a gift Augustus gave to the king of Parthia, which lay south of the Caspian Sea in Asia. [The Parthian king, Phraates IV, freed and] married Musa and gave her the name Thea Urania Musa after she had borne him a son. Musa persuaded her husband to send his older sons, along with their wives and children, to Rome [for proper educations]. . . . In 2 B.C. Musa and her son, also named Phraates, poisoned her husband. Her son took control of the kingdom and married Musa in the same year. Despite the notoriety of the marriage, Phraates V reached an accord with Augustus, and the heads of Musa and Phraates V appeared on coins.[35]

Musa's atypical experience aside, female slaves could also gain their freedom by buying it. Most Roman household slaves received a small allowance that they could spend or save, and a lady's maid sometimes received tips from her mistress's lovers or from the master for doing special favors. The slave could use this money to buy all manner of things, including extra food and clothes, luxuries, or even slaves of her own. She could also offer her master a lump sum in exchange for manumission, although he was under no obligation to agree to the deal. When a master did agree, he likely wanted to be repaid at least as much as he originally paid for the slave; he might also demand an added sum to help defray his costs for feeding and clothing her during the time he owned her.

Jobs of Freedwomen

Sadly, once a female slave achieved freedom, her life did not change all that much. The laws and customs of the Roman institution of slavery ensured that society, including her former master, still benefited from her labor without having to give her much in return. Most freeborn Romans refused to accept former slaves as complete equals, no matter how talented, loyal, or honest they might be. And freedwomen faced a number of restrictions that made them less free and of a distinctly lower status than freeborn women.

First and foremost, a freedwoman had to show her former master loyalty and social respect (*obsequium*) and was considered his social dependent. She had to do him favors from time to time; she could not sue him; and in some cases he had a legal right to half her estate if she died. Furthermore, more often than not she continued in his employ, sometimes performing the same kind of work she had done before.

Thus, many of the jobs of freedwomen were the same as those of slaves. They might be performed in the home or in a shop or small-scale factory setting. For example,

Wool Working as a Symbol of Moral Virtue

As explained here by scholars Diana E.E. Kleiner and Susan B. Matheson (from their book *I Claudia II*), Roman art came to depict wool working as symbolic of old-fashioned moral values.

Chastity was highly prized by the Romans, and they equated it in art with the act of working with wool. The story of Lucretia, as told by Livy, is a case in point. While on a military campaign, Lucretia's husband made a bet with … his comrades about the relative virtues of their wives. They hastened to Rome to see what their wives were up to in their absence. All were out carousing except the chaste Lucretia, who was at home, working her wool. Working in wool also demonstrated prudent management of the household, another wifely virtue. Funerary reliefs depicting women working in wool are meant to refer to their domestic skills. A cinerary urn … [on display] in the Metropolitan Museum of Art was used to house the remains of a woman who was prized by her husband and children for the way she tended to the home. … The loom, which traditionally stood in the house's atrium [foyer] also made reference to judicious housekeeping, and in the [wedding] procession to her new home, the bride carried the distaff and spindle.

A young, chaste Roman girl works wool using a distaff and whorl.

spinning and weaving were traditional women's household duties but professional spinning and weaving shops also existed in Rome and many other towns, making up a sort of expanded cottage industry. Six such shops have been excavated at Pompeii, so there must have been well over a hundred in Rome. Freedwomen and female slaves did all the spinning and most of the weaving in such establishments.

Spinning and weaving were merely the tip of the iceberg, for freedwomen made up a large portion of Rome's workforce at all levels. Inscriptions and other sources mention midwives, wet nurses, clothes makers, actresses, singers, dancers, musicians, mill and bakery workers, fishmongers, vegetable sellers, letter carriers, and farmworkers, among others. In addition, probably a majority of prostitutes were freedwomen. Lower-class freeborn women engaged in many of these same occupations, and sometimes it is not clear whether a woman mentioned in an inscription was a former slave or freeborn person.

A few freedwomen held more responsible or influential positions, such as landlady, moneylender, or shopkeeper. And those who worked in very wealthy households, especially the imperial palace, were clerks, secretaries, clothes folders, hairdressers, masseuses, royal attendants, and book readers, all of which were seen as prestigious positions compared to those of average working-class freedwomen and freeborn women. These higher-class freedwomen made decent wages and were known on occasion to amass small fortunes (although this was an exception to the rule).

Women in Men's Professions

Whether enslaved, freed, or freeborn, a few lower-class women even ventured into roles and occupations usually filled only by men. Scattered cases of female doctors, writers, and business owners have been documented. "Women, too, have been painters," Pliny the Elder asserted.

> Iaia of Cyzzieus, who never married, worked in Rome during the youth of Marcus Varro [in the late second and early first centuries B.C.]. She used both the painter's brush and, on ivory, the graving tool. She painted women most frequently, including a panel picture of an old woman in Naples, and even a self-portrait for which she used a mirror. No one's hand was quicker to paint a picture than hers; so great was her talent that her prices far exceeded those of the most celebrated painters of her day … whose works fill the [art] galleries. [36]

Also known are cases of women gladiators. In a society in which male gladiators were viewed as lowlife and women were supposed to "know their place," the "gladiatress" was generally seen as particularly scandalous and loathsome. Female arena fighters were far less numerous and prominent than their male counterparts. But they did come briefly into style from time to time, most notably under the emperor Domitian (reigned A.D. 81–96); he enjoyed watching women fight and paired them against male dwarves as well as against one another. Common "stage" names for female arena fighters were Achillia (a feminine form of Achilles, the warrior hero of the Greek epic poem the *Iliad*) and Amazon (a reference to the legendary race of warrior women in Greek mythology). Juvenal, whose satires ridiculed so many diverse aspects of society, was unusually hard on women gladiators:

This sculpture shows a Roman woman working in a pharmacy, a job usually filled by men. It is possible that she actually owned the establishment.

And what about female athletes, with their purple track-suits, and wrestling in the mud? Not to mention our lady-fencers [sword fighters]. We've all seen *them*, stabbing the stump with a foil [sword], shield well advanced, going through the proper motions. Just the right training needed to blow a matronly horn at the Floral Festival [held in late April and early May; all Roman festivals began with trumpet volleys]—unless they have higher ambitions, and the goal of all their practice is the real arena. But then, what modesty can be looked for in some helmeted vixen, a renegade from her sex, who thrives on masculine violence—yet would not prefer to *be* a man, since the pleasure is so much less? What a fine sight for some husband—*it might be you*—his wife's equipment put up at auction, sword-belt, armlet, plumes [helmet decorations], and one odd shin-guard! Or, if the other style of fighting takes her fancy, imagine your delight when the

A group of women crowd around a gladiator who has just performed for them at a private dinner. Though rare, female gladiators were also known.

Women of Ancient Rome

dear girl sells off her greaves [lower leg protectors]! . . . Note how she snorts at each practice thrust, bowed down by the weight of her helmet . . . then wait for the laugh, when she lays down her weapons and squats over the potty![37]

For a woman of slave or other lower-class status to become a gladiator was bad enough. But for an upper-class lady to do so was seen as especially revolting and disreputable. According to Tacitus, the ninth year of Nero's reign (A.D. 63) "witnessed gladiatorial displays on a no less magnificent scale than before, but exceeding all precedent in the number of distinguished women and senators disgracing themselves in the arena."[38]

In the early third century, the emperor Septimius Severus decided to ban female combatants from the arena. His reasoning may have been that lower-class women had plenty of opportunity to disgrace themselves in disreputable jobs like prostitute and actress; moreover, because of a long-standing tradition of male warriors, both in the army and arena, professional killing was better left to the men. This was just one more example of Roman men shaping and controlling the environment in which Roman women lived and worked.

Chapter 4:
Women in Love, Marriage, and Divorce

❧

Perhaps more than any other single aspect of life, marriage (which often involved love, having children, and sometimes divorce) preoccupied Roman women. Indeed, to a large degree, a woman's marital status and duties defined how society saw her and how she saw herself. Like the family, marriage was an ancient and respected social institution in Rome. Society also viewed it as crucial because it made one's children legitimate in the eyes of the law and the community. Marriage was always monogamous (consisting of one man and one woman), polygamy (multiple partners) being frowned on. In early Roman times, marriage was seen as so serious and sacred that divorce was virtually unknown. Eventually, though, with changing social attitudes divorce became common, especially among members of the upper classes. Love certainly played a role in both marriage and divorce, although how often and to what degree it did so remains unclear.

Arranged Marriages

The reason for this uncertainty about the role of love in Roman marriage is the lopsided nature of the evidence. Because most of the women and men described in any detail in surviving literary accounts were from the upper classes, who made up a minority of the population, it is difficult to know how most commoners felt about various aspects of life, including love. At least in upper-class society, it appears that the majority of marriages were not based on falling in love, as is the ideal today. Rather, most such unions were arranged by parents for political, social, and business reasons. And if a young woman's parents worked out a marriage deal with a prospective husband, she simply had no choice in the matter. The first-century-B.C. poet Catullus admonished a young woman not to oppose such a deal, reminding her that she was bound by law and custom to obey both her parents and her new husband:

You are not to fight with such a husband, maiden. It is not fair to fight him to whom father gave you, father himself with mother, whom you are bound to obey. Your maidenhead [virginity] is not all yours but in part your parents'; your father is given a third, your mother is given a third, [and] only a third is yours.[39]

In general, therefore, love was not seen as essential to a good marriage, or at least not as important as qualities such as obedience, loyalty, and sexual fidelity, especially on the woman's part. Still, even if passionate, romantic love was not the norm, over time society came to view mutual respect and caring as important ingredients of a successful marital union. The highly respected Musonius Rufus, who saw women as having at least the potential for equality with men, preached,

> In marriage there must be complete companionship and concern for each other on the part of both husband and wife, in health and in sickness and at all times, because they entered upon the marriage for this reason as well as to produce offspring. When such caring for one another is perfect, and the married couple provide it for one another, and each strives to outdo the other, then this is marriage as it ought to be and deserving of emulation, since it is a noble union. But when

one partner looks to his own interests alone and neglects the other's, or . . . does not wish to pull together with his partner or to cooperate, then inevitably the union is destroyed, and although they live together their common interests fare badly, and either they finally get divorced from one another or they continue on in an existence that is worse than loneliness.[40]

This fresco painting of a husband and wife was found in a house at Pompeii.

Smitten by Cupid's Arrows

Evidence shows that romantic love did exist in at least a few upper-class marriages, either from the start or perhaps growing over time. And when such love *was* the foundation of a relationship, the feelings of mutual attraction, desire, respect, and tenderness were no less profound than those experienced by modern lovers. "Love, let us live as we lived," wrote the fourth-century-A.D. poet Ausonius to his beloved wife, "nor lose the little names that were the first night's grace. And never come the day that sees us old, I still your lad, and you my little lass."[41] It seems that Pliny the Younger and his wife Calpurnia were another high-born couple smitten by Cupid's arrows. "You say that you are feeling my absence very much [as I am]," he writes to her in one of several love letters,

and your only comfort when I am not there is to hold my writings in your hand and often put them in my place by your side. I like to think that you miss me and find relief in this sort

Pliny Misses His Wife

This message (from Betty Radice's translation of Pliny's letters), written by Pliny the Younger to his wife, Calpurnia, while she was away at a health spa, shows that some Roman marriages were marked by mutual respect, caring, and love.

Never have I complained so much about my public duties as I do now. They would not let me come with you to Campania in search of better health, and they still prevent me from following hard on your heels. This is a time when I particularly want to be with you, to see with my own eyes whether you are gaining in strength and weight, and if the pleasures of your holiday and the luxuries of the district are doing you no harm. Indeed, I should worry when you are away even if you were well, for there are always anxious moments without news of anyone one loves dearly, and, as things are, I have the thought of your health as well as your absence to alarm me with fluctuating doubts and fears. I am full of forebodings of every imaginable disaster, and like all nervous people dwell most on what I pray fervently will not happen. So do please think of my anxiety and write to me once or even twice a day. I shall worry less while I am reading your letters, but my fears will return as soon as I have finished them.

of consolation. I, too, am always reading your letters, and returning to them again and again as if they were new to me. But this only fans the fire of my longing for you. If your letters are so dear to me, you can imagine how I delight in your company; do write as often as you can, although you give me pleasure mingled with pain [i.e., anxiety caused by their being apart].[42]

How common was such deep-felt love between lower-class Roman women and their husbands? Although relatively little is known about marriage among the lower classes, enough circumstantial evidence exists to draw a tentative picture. First, marrying a man with the goal of forming a political alliance or gaining noble status, so common among upper-class women, was nonexistent (or at least nearly so) among poorer ones. So, arranged marriages may have been less common. And conversely, as Pomeroy suggests, "A principal motive for marriage among the lower classes was likely to be affection."[43]

Indeed, numerous tombstone epitaphs have been found supporting the notion that common women and their husbands often formed deep bonds of love and enjoyed long, satisfying marriages. A housewife named Urbana is the subject of this touching example from the third century A.D.:

An early Roman funerary sculpture depicts an upper-class man and wife.

Sacred to the gods of the dead. To Urbana my sweetest, most chaste, and rarest wife. Surely no one more distinguished ever existed. She deserved honor also for this reason, that she lived every day of her life with me with the greatest kindness and the

"She Walked with Grace"

T his concise but moving tombstone epitaph (quoted in Mary Lefkowitz and Maureen Fant's *Women's Life in Greece and Rome*), dating from the second century B.C., honors the love and devotion of a deceased wife.

> Friends, I have not much to say; stop and read it. This tomb, which is not fair, is for a fair woman. Her parents gave her the name Claudia. She loved her husband in her heart. She bore two sons, one of whom she left on earth, the other beneath it. She was pleasant to talk with, and she walked with grace. She kept the house and worked the wool. That is all. You may go.

greatest simplicity, both in her conjugal love and the industry typical of her character. I added this so that those who read it may understand how much we loved one another. Paternus set this up in honor of his deserving wife. [44]

Equally moving is an epitaph written by a freedwoman for her departed husband, which alludes to love at first sight:

> Furia Spes, freedwoman of Sempronius Firmus, provided this memorial for her dearly beloved husband. When we were still boy and girl, we were bound by mutual love as soon as we met. I lived with him for too brief a time. We were separated by a cruel hand [death] when we should have continued to live in happiness. I therefore beg, most sacred Manes [spirits of the dead], that you look after the loved one I have entrusted to you and that you be well disposed and very kind to him during the hours of night, so that I may see him, and so that he, too, may wish to persuade fate to allow me to come to him, softly and soon. [45]

Various Kinds of Marriage

Regardless of whether a married woman was in love with her husband, law and custom held that she was still under his authority, whatever her social class. The earliest known form of Roman marital union was known as *confarreatio*. It consisted of the bride passing from her father's home (and his authority) into the house and authority (*manus*) of her new husband, so she became *in manu*, or under his control and protection almost in the same manner as his children. If she did not originally belong to his clan, she entered it on marrying him. This kind of marriage was at first engaged in mainly by members of the upper classes, and the ceremony occurred in the presence of Rome's chief priest, the *pontifex maximus*, making it sacred. (So, divorce was not an option.)

Early commoners (plebeians, or plebs) got married too, but because they were at first not full citizens, the state did not recognize their marriages. These unions were of two types. The oldest was called *usus*. *Usus* consisted of the man and woman living together continuously, perhaps for some customary period of time, and it evidently often did not involve *manus* (in which case the wife technically remained under her father's authority). The other early type of plebeian marriage was *coemptio*, a fictitious "sale" or "freeing" in which a father transferred his daughter and all of her rights to her new husband (and therefore *manus* was taken for granted).

As time went on, Roman marriage customs changed considerably. Marriage between upper- and lower-class people, for instance, which had been forbidden in the early days, became legal and eventually fairly common. At the same time, marriages

This modern drawing based on an ancient relief sculpture shows guests at a Roman wedding. As they are today, such ceremonies were filled with rituals.

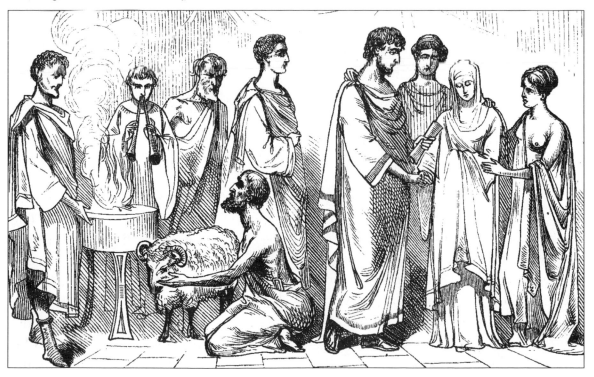

involving *manus* became increasingly less common. By the first century B.C., *usus* was no longer in use, and *confarreatio* and *coemptio* were rare. *Justae nuptiae*, which may be described as a more "regular" kind of marriage (from a modern viewpoint), had become and thereafter remained the norm.

A Roman bride's mother helps her dress for her wedding ceremony.

Such marriage required the consent of both parties; the groom had to be at least fourteen and the bride twelve (though in practice both were usually older); and marrying close relatives was forbidden. Marriage between Roman citizens and foreigners (*peregrini*) was allowed. But any children produced were citizens only if the father was; if the father was a foreigner, so were the children. Marriage between free people and former slaves had long been illegal, but in the early Empire, Augustus legalized it (although the prohibition remained for senators).

Roman Weddings

No matter what kind of marriage was involved, a ceremony sealed the union, and the bride, groom, and their family and friends took part in a wedding celebration. Typically, the couple first became betrothed, or engaged (a custom that was not obligatory). This took place at a meeting in which the parents discussed the bride's dowry (*dos*), the money or property she would bring into the marriage and from which her husband would benefit. (The money, contributed by her father, could be used by her husband. But the husband had to return it in full if they got divorced, unless he could prove his wife was guilty of immoral conduct, in which case he could keep a portion.) The meeting also included an exchange of gifts and rings and the signing of a contract (also not obligatory).

Women of Ancient Rome

Guests enjoy food and entertainment at a wedding feast. Afterward the bride accompanied the groom to his house, where he carried her over the threshold.

The actual wedding ceremony was one of the high points of a young woman's life, just as it is today. The night before the ceremony, the bride offered her childhood clothes and sometimes her toys (if she was still very young) to the family spirits at the altar in her home. The following day, the groom, his relatives, and the other guests marched in a formal procession to the bride's home, where she waited dressed in a white tunic, often an orange-red veil, and flowers in her hair. As the ceremony began, a bridesmaid stepped forward and joined the couple's hands. Commonly, the bride then recited the following words: "When and where you are, Gaius, then and there

I am Gaia," meaning "I will be at your side from now on no matter where you go." The names Gaius and Gaia were used regardless of the real names of the bride and groom, a custom dating back to Rome's dim past when Gaius was a nomen (clan name) and not a praenomen (personal name). Thus, the words in the ritual symbolized that the bride was now entering the groom's clan (indicating that this custom probably originated in the formal ceremony accompanying *confarreatio* among early Roman citizens).

After these and perhaps other words had been spoken, everyone took part in a bloodless sacrifice (of fruit or wine) to the gods and/or said a prayer to them. Then there was a feast that went on well into the evening. Finally, everyone joined in another procession, which led the bride, now a wife (*marita*), and the groom, now a husband (*maritus*), to his house. During both the feast and second procession, it was customary for the bride and her guests to sing wedding songs. None have survived, though Catullus wrote a long poem imitating their style and wording; it reads in part:

> To her home invite the mistress, hungry for her new husband, wrapping her mind round with love as clinging ivy entwines the tree, roving here and there. And you too at the same time, unwed maidens, for whom comes a like day, in tune and rhythm sing "O Hymeneal Hymen, O Hymen Hymeneal" [a reference to Hymen, a spirit thought to oversee weddings]. . . . Is any god more to be sought after by beloved lovers? Which Heavenly One will humans sooner worship, O Hymeneal Hymen, O Hymen Hymeneal? . . . And now, bridegroom, you may come. Your wife is in the bridal chamber, her face shining like a [flower]. . . . Close the doors, unmarried girls. We have played enough. But you, good wedded couple, live well and exercise your lusty youth in its constant duty![46]

When the bride reached her husband's house, he carried her over the threshold. A few close family members and friends were invited to follow them inside. There, in front of these guests, the husband offered his wife fire and water (a symbolic act welcoming her into his home) and she lit the hearth using a special marriage torch; she then threw the torch toward the guests, who scrambled to catch it, since it was thought to bring good luck. Other feasts might be held in the days that followed.

Divorce and Adultery

Despite such happy beginnings, many Roman marriages ended in divorce (*divortium*). Though divorce was fairly rare in the first few centuries of the Republic and was always initiated by the husband, by the late Republic and early Empire more liberal social attitudes and the enhanced social position of women had made divorce more common. Both women and men could now initiate it, though it was still more common for men to do so. And the procedure was now almost devoid of any social stigma. Moreover, no reasons for the breakup had to be given. The woman had the right to have her dowry returned, and in most cases the man retained custody of any children.

Evidence suggests that divorce became particularly common among the upper classes. Some modern scholars estimate

Jilted by a Freedwoman

Not all Roman marriages were happy, of course, and some ended with bad feelings. In a first-century-A.D. epitaph for his dead daughter (quoted in Lefkowitz and Fant's *Women's Life in Greece and Rome*), a father added the following curse on her mother, Acte, who had earlier left him.

> You, may your daughter's bones and your parents' rest together without you. Whatever you have done to us, may you get the same yourself. Believe me, you will be witness to your [fate]. Here are inscribed the marks of eternal shame of Acte, a freedwoman, a treacherous, tricky, hard-hearted poisoner. [I leave her] a nail and a hempen rope to fasten about her neck, and burning pitch to sear her evil heart. Manumitted gratis, she went off with an adulterer, cheated her patron, and took away his servants, a maid and a boy, as he lay in bed, leaving him a lonely, despoiled man, broken-hearted.

that as many as one-sixth of upper-class unions ended in divorce after less than ten years. In an era in which it was not unusual for a woman, particularly an upper-class one, to marry three or more times, the wry Seneca quipped,

> No woman need blush to break off her marriage since the most illustrious ladies have adopted the practice of reckoning the year . . . by [the names of] their husbands. They divorce in order to re-marry. They marry in order to divorce.[47]

One of the more common reasons for divorce was adultery (*adulterium*). But women could not cite adultery when filing for divorce because society viewed it as a given that married men could have sexual relations with mistresses, prostitutes, and slaves without fear of social stigma or recrimination. The actual frequency of adultery is not known. But it seems certain that by the dawn of the Empire it was widespread, at least in the upper classes. Poets frequently wrote about it, sometimes quite frankly, as in this witty tract by Ovid on how a woman and her lover might carry on their affair right under her husband's nose:

> So your husband will be attending the same banquet as us! I hope it will be his last supper! Am I supposed to act like a mere guest toward the woman I love? Shall I only look on,

while someone else has the pleasure of being caressed by you, while you snuggle up to him and warm his breast, while he casually puts his arm around you? . . . I'm not a wild animal, but I can scarcely keep my hands off you. Well then, pay attention and learn what you must do. . . . When your husband takes his place on the dining couch, put on an appearance of great innocence and go, as the faithful wife, to lie down beside him; but, as you pass, touch my foot without anyone's noticing. Watch me carefully, look for my nods and facial expressions. Figure out those secret unspoken messages and send me some of your own. Without speaking a word, I will tell you things by raising my eyebrows; you will read notes marked out by my fingers which are wet with wine. When memories of our lovemaking fill your mind, put your delicate finger on your rosy cheek. If you have some objection to the way I am behaving, rest your tender hand on your earlobe. When, dearest, I say or do something which pleases you, play with your ring and keep turning it with your fingers. When you are praying that some great disaster befall your husband (he deserves it), touch the table with your hand.[48]

It is important to note that if the woman Ovid describes got caught with her lover, her husband could deal with her harshly; she might be sued for divorce and lose custody of her children. By contrast, if she caught her husband with another woman, likely nothing would come of it. Women were often subject to such double standards in marital matters.

Attempts to Legislate Morality

It is not surprising, then, that women suffered more than men from a series of restrictive marriage and divorce laws initiated by Augustus in the early Empire. His goal was to restore the dignity of and respect for the institution of marriage and the integrity of the family; he felt they were being eroded by a relaxation of moral standards as reflected in the high rates of adultery and divorce. (He also wanted to raise the birthrate. It had declined significantly in the late Republic, especially among the upper classes, in part because both women and men had come to engage in sex more for fun than for having children.)

Guided by Augustus, between 18 and 9 B.C. the government passed the Lex Julia and Lex Papia Poppaea, designed to discourage adultery and encourage marriage and sexual fidelity within marriage. Under these statutes, if a man and woman were caught having an affair outside of marriage they could be dragged into public court, and if convicted suffer serious punishment. Also, the law offered rewards, such as political privileges or tax relief, to couples who stayed together and had lots of children; conversely, it carried penalties for those who did not. Unmarried adults or married couples without children lost the right to inherit money and property (except when the deceased relative was a soldier), and unmarried and childless women who owned property had to pay a special tax on that property. Other provisions in these laws that had the potential to negatively impact women included the following:

> A father is permitted, if he catches his daughter's seducer, in his own home or in his son-in-law's home ... to kill the adulterer with impunity, even as he may immediately kill his daughter.
>
> A husband is permitted to kill his wife's seducer. . . . He is permitted to kill a pimp, actor, gladiator, criminal, freedman, or slave who is caught in the act of adultery with his wife in his own home, but not in the home of his father-in-law. . . . And he must divorce his wife without delay.
>
> A husband who does not divorce his wife when she has been caught in adultery, and who allows the adulterer to go unpunished, is himself punished as a pimp.
>
> Women convicted of adultery are punished by confiscation of half of their dowry, and a third of their property, and by exile to an island.[49]

Trying to Raise Moral Standards

This provision of the Lex Julia (quoted in Elaine Fantham's *Women in the Classical World*) attempted both to keep senators from marrying lower-class women and to raise the moral standards of all Roman marriages by discouraging marriage to those kinds of women seen as disreputable.

By the Lex Julia senators and their descendants are forbidden to marry freedwomen, or women who have themselves followed the profession of the stage, or whose father or mother has done so; other freeborn persons are forbidden to marry a common prostitute, or a procuress [female pimp], or a woman manumitted by a procurer [male pimp] or procuress, or a woman caught in adultery, or one condemned in a public action, or one who has followed the profession of the stage.

It is unclear how much immediate impact these laws actually had on Roman women. Some evidence suggests that protests in aristocratic circles forced the emperor to reduce the severity of some of the penalties. But even if only a few women lost their property or ended up on an island during the Augustan era, over the longer term his attempts to legislate morality had a chilling effect; namely, they helped to *en*courage the maintenance of the social status quo and to *dis*courage the full legal emancipation of women. As Elaine Fantham puts it, the broader message these laws sent to upper-class women "was that the state would now play an ever-increasing role in their private lives and that role would symbolize the growing control by the emperor over their public lives as well."[50]

Chapter 5:
Women's Personal Lives and Habits

The duties, habits, and family roles of Roman women depended on the age in which they lived and on their wealth and social standing. In Rome's earliest centuries, for example, nearly all women, including upper-class ones, did most of the housework, cooked, spun and weaved, and made clothes. Over time, however, as upper-class families accumulated great wealth and bought and bred many slaves, the women of such families were freed from much or all menial labor. By the late Republic and early Empire, they had come to concentrate their energies more on administering their staffs of cooks, butlers, and maids; promoting the social and political interests of their children; and enjoying a wide range of leisure interests.

Meanwhile, their less fortunate counterparts—slaves, freedwomen, and poor freeborn women—continued to perform traditional women's work, much of it physically demanding. Even in the most economically expansive and socially enlightened times in Rome's history, lower-class women had little free time and had to make do with few luxuries. In the second century A.D., when the Empire was at its zenith, the Greek writer Aelius Aristides remarked in his *Roman Panegyric:* "In poor homes the same person cooks the meal, keeps the house, [and] makes the bed."[51]

Despite such differences of class and wealth, certain generalizations can be made about the personal lives and habits of most Roman women. At home they bore children, raised or oversaw the raising of their children, and had charge of the house and slaves (if any). Outside the home they walked to work (if they were lower class and had jobs), shopped in the marketplace, fetched water (if they lived on farms or in city apartment buildings, which usually lacked indoor plumbing), and went to the public baths, theater, and public games. As Rome became wealthier and more cosmopolitan in the late Republic and early Empire, women became more style conscious and desirous of creature comforts and luxuries. Many, if not most, women became preoccupied with hairdos, make-up, jewelry, and nice clothes, although only the rich could afford the best of these amenities.

Having Children

For the good of both family and community, bearing children was seen as a woman's most important personal role and duty. Without children, especially male ones, a family line would die out, a circumstance to be avoided at all costs in ancient Rome (which explains why many parents without sons adopted one). Male children were also essential to man the armies that kept the realm strong and safe. Because of women's ability to give birth, Marjorie and Benjamin Lightman point out,

Both men and women venerated and feared the sexual powers of women. The oldest priesthoods celebrated fertility. Ancient rites practiced by women assured the seasonal fertility

This seventeenth-century engraving shows a Roman woman giving birth by Caesarian section. It is unknown how often such procedures were successful.

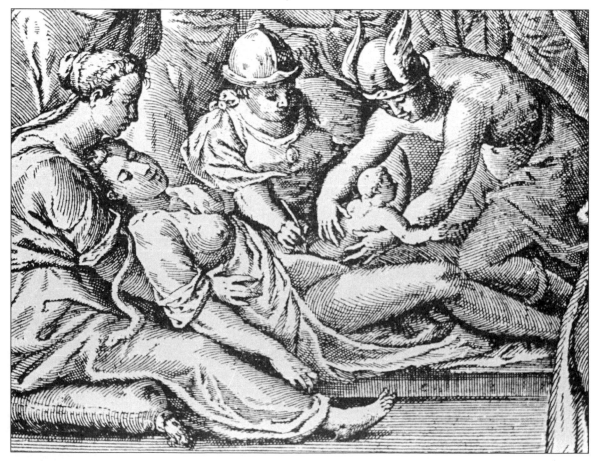

Qualities of a Good Midwife

Soranus, a second-century-A.D. Greek physician who practiced in Alexandria and Rome, wrote this tract (quoted in Jo-Ann Shelton's *As the Romans Did*) about what an expectant couple should look for in a midwife.

We label someone "the best midwife" . . . particularly if she is trained in all branches of therapy (for some cases require special diet, some require surgery, some must be treated with drugs) and is able to prescribe hygienic rules, to observe both general and individual symptoms, and to discover from them what needs to be done. . . . She will be calm and unruffled in crises, and able to give a clear account of the procedures she is using. She will provide reassurance to her patients and will be sympathetic . . . She will be prudent and always sober, since she is never sure when she will be summoned to a woman in danger. She will be discreet since she will share in many secrets of life. . . . She will not be superstitious and will not overlook a possible remedy because of a dream or an omen.

of childbirth, and . . . fertility of the land. This power was . . . praised in every eulogy written by men about women. No [female] glory was greater than to bear children. [52]

As was true across the ancient world, Roman women had their children at home, delivered by midwives. Some idea of a midwife's duties and methods, along with the birth process itself, comes from this fascinating excerpt from a first-century-A.D. treatise on gynecology:

For normal childbirth, have the following ready: oil for injections [into the vagina as a lubricant] and cleansing, hot water in order to wash the affected area, hot compresses to relieve the labor pains, sponges for sponging off; wool for covering the woman's body, and bandages to swaddle [wrap] the baby in, a pillow so that the infant may be placed on it below the mother until the afterbirth [placenta] has been taken away . . . a birthing stool so that the mother may be arranged on it . . . two couches, the one made up with soft coverings for rest after giving birth, the other hard for lying down on between labor pains. . . . When the mouth of the womb is open, and the midwife has

Calpurnia's Miscarriage

In this letter to his wife's grandfather, Calpurnius Fabatus, Pliny the Younger reveals the sad news that Calpurnia has had a miscarriage.

I know how anxious you are for us to give you a great-grandchild, so you will be all the more sorry to hear that your granddaughter has had a miscarriage. Being young and inexperienced she did not realize she was pregnant, failed to take proper precautions, and did several things which were better left undone. She has had a severe lesson, and paid for her mistake by seriously endangering her life; so that although you must inevitably feel it hard for your old age to be robbed of a descendant already on the way, you should thank the gods for sparing your granddaughter's life even though they denied you the child for the present.

washed her hands with hot oil, she should put in her forefinger . . . of her left hand, and by gently drawing it arrange the opening [in preparation for the delivery]. . . . Three women should stay ready who are able gently to calm the fears of the woman who is giving birth, even if they do not happen to have experience in childbirth. . . . The midwife should then sit holding her thighs apart and with her left thigh leaning to support her left hand, in front of the mother. . . . If the amniotic sac remains unbroken for a long time, she should break it with her fingernails and put her fingers in it and little by little open it wider. She should take care that the infant not fall out at once. . . . When the infant tries to come out, the midwife should have a cloth in her hands to pick him up.[53]

Unfortunately, people in those days did not know about germs and how they cause infections, and prenatal and postnatal care were primitive by today's standards. So, rates of miscarriage and of both infants and mothers dying in childbirth were much higher than in modern times. (Exact rates are unknown. But modern scholars estimate that between 10 and 20 percent of pregnant women died in childbirth, as compared to about .01 percent in the United States today; in addition, 25 percent or more of children died before age one, as compared to less than 1 percent in the United States today.) Moreover, such tragedies cut across class lines, probably striking the well-to-do as often as the poor. Julius Caesar's daughter, Julia, suffered a miscarriage and a year later died while giving birth; Nero's daughter, his only child, died a few months after her birth; and Pliny the Younger bemoaned the miscarriages and deaths of friends' daughters. "This premature death of Helvidius's daughters is tragic—both sisters giving birth to girls and dying in labor," he wrote in one of his letters.

I am deeply distressed, and not unduly, for those were noble young women in the flower of their youth and I must mourn to see them the victims of their motherhood. I grieve, too, for the plight of their infants left motherless at birth. . . . Now only one of his three children survives, left as the sole prop and stay of a family which not so long ago had many members to support it.[54]

Mother-Child Relationships

As for the relationship between those mothers and children who survived, evidence is sketchy and biased by the absence of literary accounts by women. Noted classical scholar Jo-Ann Shelton writes,

When Roman writers do describe their mothers, they generally present us with an idealized portrait of a Roman matron, a woman who is virtuous, strong, self-sacrificing, and devoted to the education and political advancement of her family. But we seldom hear of real warmth in the mother-child relationship. Roman writers, when they mention their mothers at all (which is rare), seem to worship them from a distance. There are various explanations for this apparent lack of warmth. Since many women died young, often in childbirth, their children may never have known them. A man might be married two or three times and his children would thus be raised by stepmothers. In cases of divorce, moreover, children remained with their father, not their mother, and they might not see her again. In addition, many upper-class Roman children were raised by nurses or nannies and might therefore feel more love toward the nurses who had fed, bathed, and clothed them than toward their mothers. Yet surely many Romans loved their mothers dearly, and perhaps it was strictly literary convention which led them to describe their mothers in terms of generalized virtues rather than to recall personal and highly individual memories of maternal warmth.[55]

Conversely, Roman mothers almost certainly had strong maternal feelings of love and affection, even if in many cases stepmothers or nurses ended up actually raising the children. It is important to emphasize that in Roman society mothers were not necessarily seen as the primary nurturers and caregivers, as modern women are. Shelton's mention of children's education and social advancement is key.

The ancient sculpture on which this drawing was based attempted to show the ideal Roman matron—virtuous, dignified, and well-groomed.

The economic, social, and professional betterment of her children seems to have been a mother's primary task in child rearing, regardless of social class. "For daughters, this meant arranging advantageous marriages," Diane Kleiner and Susan Matheson point out.

> For sons the goal was political and economic advancement, whether through marriage, a military campaign, a foreign service post, a high public office, and preferably all of these, and mothers as well as fathers devoted every possible effort to their sons' success. We see this maternal drive in imperial women such as [Augustus's wife] Livia and [Nero's mother] Agrippina the Younger. . . . Family advancement and family unity were also the goals of Roman freedwomen who commissioned [funerary] monuments that publicly expressed their pride in their children's upward climb in what was a mobile Roman society.[56]

Clothes and Hairdos

While a woman's duties benefited her children, husband, family and home, she also developed habits and accumulated personal items that benefited herself. Most women enjoyed looking their best. And wearing nice clothes, or at least clothes appropriate to various situations, was essential. The most common casual garment was the simple tunic, worn both indoors and outdoors, depending on the occasion or one's social status. The tunic was made from two rectangular pieces of cloth stitched up the sides, with holes cut for the head and arms. Women wore it knee-length and usually wore an ankle-length dress, the *stola,* over it. Rich women wore *stolae* of silk or other fine materials, while commoners settled for linen or wool. When leaving the house, most women also wore a large shawl, the *palla.* In early Roman times the polite custom was to cover their heads with the *palla,* but by the advent of the Empire it was acceptable not to. For undergarments, women wore loincloths and cloth bras (*fasciae*) and corsets.

In addition to these basic types of clothes, women, at least those who could afford it, wore cloaks, scarves, and capes, when fashion or the weather dictated. Decorative fastening pins called *fibulae* held cloaks, scarves, and other garments in place at the shoulder. In extremely casual surroundings, such as the public baths or the beach, many women wore tunics and pantslike bottoms; surviving paintings also show that a few sported bikinis similar to those seen today.

For many Roman women, the proper clothes had to be accented by the proper hairstyle. In the early Republic the most common style was long hair gathered up in a simple bun or knot in the back and

The woman in the middle wears a stola *with a* palla *draped over it.*

held in place by a hairpin; later, as women became more socially liberated and fashion conscious, they adopted a wide range of styles, including creatively curled and styled hairdos, many of which are seen in surviving busts and paintings. Some women also dyed their hair or wore hairpieces and wigs. Blond and red were the preferable colors. The dye was a concoction imported from the Rhine region of western Germany; the hair for wigs came from slaves or war captives, again from Germany.

Interestingly, there was more to women's hairdos in Rome than mere fashion and

These drawings, based on surviving Roman portrait busts, show some of the more popular hairstyles sported by women in the early Empire.

vanity. To a certain degree, a woman's beauty was perceived as a feminine virtue as much as a physical quality. Kleiner and Matheson explain:

A woman with an exquisite hairstyle was at once attractive and also virtuous. Empresses and princesses worked with their hairstylists to create new coiffures because they wanted to be perceived as fashionable, on the cutting edge, and prosperous, but, at the same time, these hairstyles proclaimed that their wearer possessed all the traits desirable in the ideal Roman woman. . . . Livia's hairstyle was copied in large part because it was hers and she was empress of Rome. But it was also imitated because it literally had bound up with it all the desirable features of ideal Roman womanhood, enumerated in the Augustan marriage and moral legislation. . . . Livia wore the simple hairstyle as a statement that she, unlike Cleopatra [queen of Egypt], her husband's foe at [the Battle of] Actium, was a woman of high moral character . . . not a foreign woman given to what was reported to be ostentatious [overly showy] excess. . . . When aris-

Women of Ancient Rome

tocratic women, freedwomen, and even female slaves adopted Livia's hairstyle, they did so . . . [partly] to indicate that they possessed the same virtues as their imperial counterparts and that they were Romans. [57]

Makeup and Jewelry

Many Roman women also wore makeup, although exactly who did so and how often is unclear. At first, apparently mostly prostitutes and actresses wore it, but by the first century B.C. makeup had become fashionable for any woman who could afford it. Nevertheless, society retained a hard core of old-fashioned or puritanical types who viewed makeup as gaudy and low class, as reflected in highly critical, sarcastic, or unkind remarks by some male writers, notably satirists like Juvenal and the second-century-A.D. Greek, Lucian of Samosata. (Unfortunately, no writings by women defending the use of makeup have survived.) As Lucian put it,

If you saw women getting out of bed in the morning, you would find them more repulsive than monkeys. That is why they shut themselves up and refuse to be seen by a man [until they get their makeup on]; old hags and a troupe of servant-maids as ugly as their mistress surround her, plastering her unhappy face with a variety of ointments. For a woman does not just

wash away her sleepiness with cold water, and proceed to a serious day's work. No, innumerable concoctions in the way of salves are used to brighten her unpleasing complexion. As in a public process, each of the servants has some different object in her

Typical female grooming items, including mirrors, hairpins, comb, and perfumes.

hand; a silver basin, a jug, a mirror, a multitude of boxes, enough to stock a chemist's shop, jars full of mischief, tooth powders [to make the teeth look whiter] or stuff for blackening the eyelids. [58]

What exactly were in these "jars full of mischief"? First, women used a chalklike powder or sometimes white lead to make their complexions pale, which was considered stylish. They also painted their lips and cheeks red, and lined their eyes and eyebrows with black *stibium* (powdered antimony mixed with water). Martial poked fun at one woman's artificial look, saying,

Your tresses [a wig], Galla, are manufactured far away [in Germany] . . .

and you lie [sleep] stored away in a hundred caskets [cosmetics boxes] . . . and your face does not sleep with you, yet you wink [at men] with that eyebrow which has been brought out [of a drawer by your servant] for you in the morning. [59]

Indeed, the makeup tables of many Roman women were crammed with razors, brushes, hairnets, wigs, and jars of creams, pastes, oils, colored dyes, and perfumes. In addition, some women carried a "pocket set," or portable grooming kit, usually on a ring attached to their belts when away from home. A typical set contained, in addition to various makeup items, tweezers, a nail cleaner, an ear cleaner similar to a modern Q-tip, and a toothpick.

Too Many Cosmetics?

Juvenal is famous for his invective about society's ills, in this case (from his sixth satire) women who use too many cosmetics, perfumes, and other beauty products.

What's more insufferable than your well-heeled female? But earlier in the process she presents a sight as funny as it's appalling, her features lost under a damp bread face-pack, or greasy with vanishing-cream that clings to her husband's lips when the poor man kisses her, though it's all wiped off for her lover. She takes no trouble about the way she looks at home. Those imported Indian scents and lotions she buys with a lover in mind. First one layer, then the next. At last the contours emerge till she's almost recognizable. . . . But all these medicaments and various treatments—not least the damp bread-poultice—make you wonder what's underneath, a face or an ulcer.

Women of Ancient Rome

As for jewelry, Roman women of all social classes had a passionate fondness for it. In the early Republic, their use of jewelry was more modest, partly because social customs tended to be more conservative and austere; also, precious metals and gems were less common and only upper-class women were allowed to wear gold rings. In later republican times, however, when Rome absorbed the Greek east, more liberal attitudes and styles and the ready availability of precious metals and gems made the wearing of a wide range of jewelry a must for the fashionable Roman woman.

In ancient Rome, as in modern societies, the most common types of jewelry included gold chains, bracelets, and anklets; strings of pearls; rings with precious gems set in gold or silver; earrings of gold, silver, bronze, pearl, and/or emerald; and decorative hairpins, brooches, medallions, and cameos (made by carving a face or other subject in relief on the surface of a gem or small stone). The richest women owned priceless collections of jewelry. According to Pliny the Elder, for example, Lollia Paulina, the emperor Caligula's wife, had a single set of pearls and emeralds (consisting of a necklace, ring, crown, and earrings) worth 40 million sesterces, a huge sum. People also commonly dedicated valuable jewelry items to goddesses and adorned their statues with them. By contrast, poorer women had to content themselves largely with jewelry made of nonprecious metals and fake gems fashioned of colored glass.

Dinner Parties

Having donned a comely outfit, fixed her hair, and applied makeup and jewelry, a well-groomed woman was ready to receive guests, give or attend a dinner party, or venture out in public. Various surviving sources reveal that Roman women dined and socialized with dinner guests at home (as compared to most Greek women, who were kept away from male visitors) and went to dinner parties with their husbands at the homes of friends and social contacts. In one source, the first-century-B.C. Roman biographer Cornelius Nepos tells how, on a visit to Athens, he found the Greek segregation of women odd in comparison to the customs of his own society:

Many actions are acceptable according to our Roman code which the Greeks look upon as shameful. For instance, what Roman would blush to take his wife to a dinner-party? What matron does not frequent the front rooms of her dwelling and show herself in public? But it is very different in [Athens]; for there a woman is not admitted to a dinner party, unless relatives only are present, and she keeps to the more retired part of the house called "the women's apartment," to which no man has access who is not near of kin. [60]

In the late Republic and early Empire, well-to-do Roman men regularly took their wives to posh dinner parties like the one in this reconstruction.

In a well-to-do Roman home, which had a large staff of slaves, the lady of the house neither prepared nor served the meal (although she might choose which dishes would be served). Instead, she took her place at a large table in the dining room (*triclinium*) and enjoyed the meal and enter-tainment, if any. (Larger or special gather-ings might feature singers, dancers, acrobats, or wrestlers.) By custom she sat upright in a chair, while her husband reclined on a small couch, until the late first century B.C. when women began to recline at meals along with men. Evidence suggests that women in upper-class circles drank sparingly at such gatherings, since society frowned on female drunkenness. (Whether commoners drank more or were more likely to become intoxicated is unknown.) Also, women freely conversed with men at meals; the works of Roman men contain references to upper-class women who were excellent conversationalists. However, the prudent woman was probably careful not to appear more educated or better informed than her husband and his male friends, as many men apparently found this irritating or threatening.

Outings and Their Restrictions

On excursions outside the house, women went to the public baths, the marketplace and various shops, friends' or patrons' houses, religious ceremonies and funerals, the theater, gladiatorial combats and wild beast fights, and the chariot races. Upper-class women were usually accompanied by a male relative and/or a retinue of servants (to show off their wealth and status). Yet women of all social classes sometimes appeared in public with only one or two servants or girlfriends. Such outings were opportunities to meet men, especially at large gathering places, such as the Circus Maximus, where chariot races were held. In the following charming passage, Ovid describes an attempted romantic encounter with an attractive young woman at the racetrack:

I'm not sitting here because of my enthusiasm for horse races; but I will pray that the chariot driver you favor may win. I came here, in fact, so that I might sit beside you and talk to you. I didn't want the love which you stir in me to be concealed from you. So you watch the races, and I'll watch you. Let's each watch the things we love most, and let's feast our eyes on them. . . . Why are you edging away from me? It's no use. The seat marker forces us to touch. Yes, the Circus does offer some advantages in its seating rules. Hey, you on the right, whoever you are, be more considerate of the lady! . . . Draw in your legs, if you have any sense of decency, and don't stick your bony knees in her back. Oh dear, your skirt is trailing a bit on the ground. Lift it up, or here, I will do it. . . . (But what will happen when I see her ankles? Even when they were hidden I burned with passion. Now I am adding flames to the fire. . . . From the sight of her ankles, I can well imagine the other delights which lie carefully hidden under her clothing.) Would you like me to stir a light breeze by using my program as a fan?[61]

Despite the fact that women attended such events, their access to many public areas and venues was not nearly as free and easy as it was for men. Although a young woman had the legal right to walk the streets without a chaperone, servants, or friends, she might have to get a male relative's permission. And she ran the risk of men making passes at her at every turn, some probably not as polite as the one Ovid described, since an unescorted woman was at the least suspected of having loose morals.

In addition, the government sometimes felt obliged to protect women from potentially "disturbing" or "lewd" displays. The most often cited case was Augustus's moral legislation, some of which restricted women at public games. According to his edicts, women attending gladiatorial shows had to sit in the upper parts of the amphitheater so that they could not see

This modern drawing of spectators at a Roman chariot race recalls the romantic setting of Ovid's flirtation with a young woman at the Circus Maximus.

Women of Ancient Rome

the bloodshed up close, and he completely excluded women from Greek-style athletic contests in which men competed nude or wearing very little. This shows how women's life was in large part shaped by men who felt compelled to guard against "the process of our moral decline," as Livy put it in the preface to his famous history. "Watch [out for] the sinking of the foundations of morality," he warned, "and the dark dawning of our modern day, when we can neither endure our vices nor face the remedies needed to cure them." [62]

Chapter 6:
Religious Roles and Rites of Roman Women

"It might be said that Rome subordinated its goddesses as it subordinated its women," [63] Elaine Fantham observes. Indeed, though the Romans worshiped many female deities, all of these goddesses were subject to the authority of a male god—Jupiter, head of the official state pantheon (group of gods). Just as the paterfamilias held ultimate power over the members of his family, Jupiter dominated the family of gods. Included were his wife, Juno, a protector of marriage; Minerva, originally a patron of arts and crafts but later a war goddess as well; Vesta, goddess of the hearth; Venus, goddess of love; and others. In this way, the workings of the divine realm conveniently mirrored the realities of Roman life.

This does not mean that these and other goddesses worshiped at Rome were unimportant or that Roman women did not play a significant role in religion. In fact, appeasing Vesta was seen as essential to the well-being of the state. In times of crisis—for example, when the Romans were disastrously defeated by Hannibal of Carthage in 216 B.C.—many leaders suspected that Vesta was displeased by corruption among her priestesses, the Vestal Virgins. Only by punishing those guilty of such wrongdoing could Rome win back the goddess's favor.

At the same time, Roman women, whose lives were legally and socially restricted in numerous ways, could find in religious worship and duties a measure of joy, release, and feelings of self-esteem. Priestesses, especially the Vestals and a few others, were widely respected and, in comparison to other women, highly privileged. Moreover, even ordinary women experienced a sense of purpose, prestige, and communal sisterhood by taking part in several religious festivals from which men were excluded.

A Goddess's Many Sides

Roman women did not all worship together as a single group or on an equal basis, however. The same economic, class, and other distinctions that divided women in society at large also prevailed in most religious matters. Separate cults (each cult consisting of the shrines, worshipers, and worship of a god) were created for the various social ranks. Thus, for any given god there might be a cult for female patricians (the aristocratic landholding class); one for plebeian women who were seen as respectable; and another for less reputable plebeian women (prostitutes, actresses, and so forth). Other cults discriminated according to a particular status, such as married versus unmarried; slave versus free; and the number of husbands a woman had had. (A *univira*, a woman who had been with only one man in her life, was seen as the ideal and could belong to an exclusive cult.)

Consider, for example, Fortuna, an ancient fertility goddess linked with female maturation and sexual fulfillment. (She eventually came to be identified with Tyche, the Greek deity of fate, chance, or luck, and thereby gained a wider following.) Both men and women worshiped Fortuna in a major annual public festival. Large numbers of people rowed or walked

The white-clad Vestal Virgins perform a religious sacrifice in this painting based on an image on a Roman coin. The Vestals constituted a very ancient priesthood.

to her principal shrine, located about a mile downstream from Rome, and after watching the ceremonies, they held picnics and feasts.

However, the goddess had many other shrines in Rome and other Roman cities. And various groups of women addressed or worshiped her by a wide variety of names, each name representing the side of her character that oversaw a specific group. There was Fortuna Virginalis, for instance, who looked after young virgin girls, and Fortuna Primigenia of Praeneste, who protected mothers and childbirth. Fortuna Virginalis had a temple in Rome's busy cattle market, and the cult of Patrician Chastity, exclusively for patrician *univirae*, came to associate itself with this manifestation of the goddess. Among the other Fortuna cults were those of Plebeian Chastity, open only to plebeian *univirae*, and Fortuna Virilis, for slaves and other lower-class women. (Fortuna Virilis was also called Fortuna Balnearis, "of the

The Temple of Fortuna as it may have appeared in late republican times, after being rebuilt at least twice. Note the altar at the bottom of the staircase.

Women of Ancient Rome

baths," because the worshipers gathered in public bathhouses.)

This rigid class snobbery that pervaded Rome's female ranks (as well as the male ones) is well illustrated by the manner in which the cult of Plebeian Chastity came into being in 296 B.C. A member of the cult of Patrician Chastity, Verginia, had recently married a plebeian, Lucius Volumnius. Though he had recently risen to the prestigious rank of consul, the patrician women felt that Verginia had demeaned herself by marrying below her class. So they attempted to keep her from worshiping at the patrician shrine. According to Livy,

> A short altercation followed, which when feminine tempers ran high, blazed out into a battle of wills. Verginia proudly insisted and with reason, that she had entered the temple of Patrician Chastity as a patrician and a chaste woman, who was the wife of one man [i.e., a *univira*], to whom she had been given as an unmarried girl and was ashamed neither of her husband nor of his honors and achievements. Then she confirmed her noble words by a remarkable deed. In the Vicus Longus, where she lived, she shut off part of her great house, large enough to make a shrine of moderate size, set up an altar in it, and then summoned the married plebeian women. After

complaining about the insulting behavior of the patrician ladies, "I dedicate this altar," she said, "to Plebeian Chastity, and urge you to ensure that it will be said that it is tended more reverently than any other one, if that is possible, and by women of purer life. Thus, just as the men in our state are rivals in valor, our matrons may compete with one another in chastity." [64]

Public and Private Ceremonies

The festivals and ceremonies of many exclusive women's cults were private. Because men were not allowed to take part, or even to watch, male writers did not record the details of what went on at these gatherings; therefore, this information is mostly lost. But a reasonably clear picture of women's roles and activities in public religious festivals has survived. Most public worship in ancient Rome involved sacred processions in which people marched through the streets, dressed in fine clothes and often singing hymns; prayer; feasts; and most important, sacrifice of plants, wine, and/or animals at altars (which were usually located outside, on the grounds of temples). Livy provides a description of women leading cows to sacrifice in honor of the goddess Juno:

> The order of the ceremony was as follows. From the temple of Apollo

The ruins of the Temple of Juno (left), in a Roman town in North Africa. Local religious processions honoring the goddess ended up in front of this edifice.

two white cows were led into the city through the Porta Carmentalis [one of the city's main gates]; behind them were carried two images, in cypress wood, of Queen Juno, then twenty-seven virgins in long robes followed, singing a hymn to Juno. . . . The virgins were followed by the decemvirs [state officials] wearing laurel wreaths and togas with a purple border. The procession passed from the gate . . . to the Forum [main square]; there it halted, and the virgins, all taking hold of a rope, moved forward again keeping time with the rhythm of their hymn. From the Forum the procession [moved through the city] . . . to the temple of Queen Juno, where the two cows were offered in sacrifice.[65]

Private, exclusive female cults no doubt engaged in some of these same activities. Hymn singing, prayer, and sacrifice were probably essential elements. Some evidence suggests that women who took part in such ceremonies also viewed or handled certain objects sacred to a particular goddess.

One of ancient Rome's most famous scandals concerned a man who may have seen such sacred objects that were meant only for women's eyes. The incident took place in 63 B.C. and involved Publius Clodius Pulcher, a patrician with a shady reputation. As Plutarch tells it, Clodius was in love with Pompeia, Julius Caesar's wife. That year the private rites of Bona Dea (the so-called good goddess), a fertility deity worshiped almost exclusively by women, were held in Caesar's and Pompeia's house. (The custom was to hold the ceremony at the home of one of the serving consuls; the men of the house vacated the premises for the day.) Hoping to pay a secret visit to Pompeia while her husband was away, Clodius dressed up like a woman, wig and all, and that night one of Pompeia's maids admitted him. The man unwisely began to wander from room to room, perhaps seeing things forbidden to men, and eventually a servant of Aurelia, Caesar's mother, saw through Clodius's disguise. The servant "shrieked and ran off," Plutarch wrote,

crying out that she had caught a man. The women were in a panic. Aurelia put a stop to the sacred rites of the goddess and covered up the holy things. She then ordered the doors to be shut and went all over the house with lighted torches in search of Clodius. He was found hiding in the room belonging to the maid who had let him into the house and, when it was discovered who he was, the women drove him out of doors. They

The Great Mother

Besides Isis, Cybele was the most popular female deity imported from the East in late republican times. She originated in Phrygia (in west-central Asia Minor) and eventually became extremely popular across much of the Mediterranean world. Cybele was a fertility deity who came to be seen as a life-giving ancient mother; hence she came to be known as the "Great Mother." People also thought she could cure (or if angry, inflict) disease and protect people in wartime. Her male consort, Attis, was later worshiped along with her. The Romans began worshiping Cybele in 204 B.C., near the close of the Second Punic War. At that time, a Roman ambassador journeyed to Phrygia and brought her sacred black stone (supposedly a meteorite) back to Rome, where a few years later it was installed in a temple built to her on the Palatine Hill. During the first century A.D., Cybele's festival, the Megalesia, celebrated from April 4 to 10, became popular throughout the Roman Empire.

then went away immediately while it was still night and told their husbands what had happened. As soon as it was day then word was going about the city that Clodius had committed sacrilege and owed satisfaction not only to those who had been outraged by his conduct, but also to the city and the gods. One of the tribunes, therefore, officially indicted Clodius for sacrilege and the most influential members of the Senate banded themselves together against him. [66]

Political Manipulation of Religion

There is no way to know how many Romans actually believed Clodius had committed sacrilege or worried about the goddess's wrath. What is certain is that the incident turned into a political affair. Clodius's powerful enemies tried to take advantage of his indiscretion to discredit him, but he retained many supporters among the common people. Ultimately he was acquitted and Caesar divorced Pompeia so that his own political career would not be tainted.

Another incident involving the same goddess shows how powerful politicians could manipulate a deity's cult and priestesses to justify controversial political decisions and actions. During the crisis over Catiline's failed plot to take over the government, Cicero shrewdly took advantage of the simple flare-up of a fire to enlist divine support for dealing harshly with the conspirators. "It was now evening," Plutarch wrote,

and the people were waiting outside in dense crowds. Cicero came out of the Senate . . . and was escorted by [some friends] to the house of a neighboring friend of his, since his own house was taken up by the women who were celebrating the secret rites in honor of the goddess [Bona Dea]. . . . Sacrifices are offered to her annually in the house of the consul and are supervised by the consul's wife or mother in the presence of the Vestal Virgins. Cicero therefore went to his friend's house and began to consider in his own mind . . . what action he should take with regard to the conspirators. . . . [Meanwhile] a sign was given to the women who were sacrificing. The fire on the altar was assumed to have already gone out, but from the ashes and burned bark a great bright flame sprang up. It was a sight which terrified most of the women, but the sacred virgins told Cicero's wife Terentia to go at once to her husband and tell him to act as he had decided to act for the good of his country, since the goddess was sending him a great light to

The Good Goddess

Bona Dea, the "good goddess," into whose rites Clodius intruded in his attempt to visit Pompeia, was a fertility deity worshiped almost exclusively by women. The Romans sometimes identified Bona Dea with another goddess of fertility, Fauna, and celebrated her festival annually on December 3. In her only myth, her father, the agricultural god Faunus, raped her after getting her drunk. This was said to be the reason that wine was banned from her ceremonies.

A priestess of Bona Dea, the "good goddess," worships that deity while the Vestal Virgins look on. Men were banned from such ceremonies.

promise him both safety and glory. Terentia was never at any time a shrinking type of woman; she was bold and energetic by nature, ambitious, and, as Cicero says himself, was more inclined to take a part in his public life than to share with him any of her domestic responsibilities. So she now delivered the message and urged him to take action against the conspirators.[67]

The Sibyls

Even though holy women (and holy men as well) could be manipulated by powerful leaders, Roman priestesses were widely respected and revered because they were seen as having special connections to various divinities. One of the most ancient of these special women was called a Sibyl, who was thought to have prophetic powers. There were various Sibyls in various times and places, many of whom had individual names. Their prophecies were supposedly delivered when they were possessed by Apollo, god of prophecy and healing. People wrote down what Sibyls said when in this state and later collected these writings.

The most famous example, the Sibylline Books, consisted of the prophecies of the most important of all Roman Sibyls— the one who resided at Cumae, in southwestern Italy. According to the poet Virgil, it was she who took Aeneas, founder of the Roman race, into the Underworld and showed him Rome's glorious future. The later Romans consulted the Sibylline Books from time to time, partly for guidance in making future plans and policies. They also consulted them to find out how to appease angry gods who had, it was thought, caused disasters such as earthquakes and plagues. The books were stored in a chest in a chamber beneath Jupiter's temple on the Capitoline Hill in Rome. Presumably they were lost when the temple was destroyed in the fifth century A.D. (Many early Christians came to view the Sibyls

A seventeenth-century Italian painting depicts the Sibyl of Cumae.

as equivalent to Old Testament prophets and portrayed them that way in Christian art and literature.)

The Vestals

Though Sibyls were famous and revered, undoubtedly the most important Roman priestesses were the Vestal Virgins. In very ancient days there were only two Vestals, a number that eventually increased to four and then six. Their main duties were to watch over the sacred fire on the state hearth in the Temple of Vesta and to care for the sacred objects kept in the temple. They also made a special salt cake used in various religious festivals throughout the year. According to Plutarch, their obligations and privileges were as follows:

> They should take a vow of virginity for the space of thirty years, the first ten of which they were to spend in learning their duties, the second ten in performing them, and the remaining ten in teaching and instructing others. Thus the whole term being completed, it was lawful for them to marry, and, leaving the sacred order, to choose any condition of life that pleased them; but this permission few . . . made use of; and in cases where they did so, it was observed that their

The ruins of the Temple of Vesta, excavated in the late nineteenth century and partially reconstructed in 1930, stand in Rome's main Forum.

change was not a happy one, but accompanied ever after with regret and melancholy; so that the greater number, from religious fears and scruples, forbore [getting married], and continued to old age and death in the strict observance of a single life. For this condition [the Vestals were] compensated by great privileges and prerogatives; as that they had power to make a will in the lifetime of their father; that they had a free adminis-tration of their own affairs without guardian or tutor. . . . When they go abroad, they have the fasces [symbols of Roman power] carried before them; and if in their walks they chance to meet a criminal on his way to execution, it saves his life, upon oath made that the meeting was an accidental one. . . . Anyone who presses upon the chair [litter] on which they are carried, is put to death. [68]

During their first ten years in the priesthood, the Vestals learned to execute their duties. This nineteenth-century painting depicts their school.

Women of Ancient Rome

The Vestals were chosen by Rome's chief priest, the *pontifex maximus,* from a pool of aristocratic girls age six to ten. The second-century-A.D. Roman writer Aulus Gellius explained which of the young women in this age group were exempted from serving as Vestals:

It is unlawful to take a girl . . . whose father and mother are not living, or who has a speech or hearing defect, or any other bodily imperfection. She must not have been freed from her father's power, even if her father is alive and she is in the power of her grandfather; likewise, neither of her parents must ever have been slaves nor held lowly occupations. But they say that she is exempt if her sister was elected to the priesthood; likewise if her father is a [priest]. . . . Also exempt are girls who are betrothed to a [priest]. . . . Moreover . . . the daughter of a man who does not have a residence in Italy cannot be chosen, and the daughter of a man who has three children is to be excused. [69]

Maintained at state expense, the Vestals dwelled in a house called the Hall of Vesta, located near the main Forum, and wore plain white linen dresses. The white both symbolized and emphasized their purity. Indeed, that sexual purity was their most important asset and duty. If a Vestal was found guilty of being unchaste, she was buried alive in a small underground chamber and her lover was beaten to death. The execution of a Vestal was a national tragedy and so rare that fewer than a dozen of these priestesses met this fate in the entire course of Rome's history.

Cults of Ceres and Isis

Although not as prestigious as the Vestals, priestesses of the cult of Ceres also administered an important state cult and enjoyed wide respect. Ceres was a very ancient Italian goddess of grain who personified nature's yearly renewal and regeneration. In addition, she was a guardian of the dead, and people often sacrificed to her after a funeral to purify the house of the deceased. Both men and women celebrated her popular festival, the Cerialia, from April 12 to 19.

Beginning in the late third century B.C., the Romans began identifying Ceres with the Greek fertility goddess Demeter and a new, female-only cult of Ceres was created. Its priestesses were Greek women who were invited to Rome and granted Roman citizenship. Their rites were secret, but it is believed that they involved reenactments of the principal myth of Ceres/Demeter, in which the goddess frantically searched for her daughter, who had been abducted by the lord of the Underworld.

In addition to the age-old Greco-Roman deities worshiped at Rome, in the

The Execution of a Vestal

In this excerpt from his biography of one of Rome's early kings, Numa (John Dryden's translation), Plutarch gives some of the details about the grim penalty a Vestal received for losing her virginity.

A Vestal is buried alive as a punishment for breaking her vows.

She that has broken her vow is buried alive near the gate called Collina, where a little mound of earth stands. . . . Under it a narrow room is constructed, to which a descent is made by stairs; here they prepare a bed, and light a lamp, and leave a small quantity of food, such as bread, water, a pail of milk, and some oil; so that body which had been consecrated and devoted to the most sacred service of religion might not be said to perish by such a death as famine. The culprit herself is put in a litter, which they cover over, and tie her down with cords on it, so that nothing she utters may be heard. They then take her to the Forum; all people silently go out of the way as she passes, and . . . [some follow, expressing] solemn and speechless sorrow; and indeed, there is not any spectacle more appalling, nor any day observed by the city with greater appearance of gloom and sadness. When they come to the place of execution, the officers loose the cords, and then the high priest . . . brings out the prisoner . . . and placing her upon the steps that lead down to the cell, turns away his face. . . . The stairs are drawn up after she has gone down, and a quantity of earth is heaped up over the entrance to the cell. . . . This is the punishment of those who break their vow of virginity.

This exquisite Roman statue of Isis dates from the early Empire.

late Republic a number of cults of foreign goddesses were imported from the eastern Mediterranean and Near East. Among these goddesses were Cybele, from Asia Minor; Atargatis, from Syria; and Isis, from Egypt. Isis was seen as having many pow-ers and talents, perhaps the most important being her fertility, healing powers, motherly attributes, and promise to grant her worshipers resurrection and salvation after death. Isis was also a patron of navigation and commerce. Her cult became particularly popular among women partly because her worship was open to all—men, women, slaves, freedwomen, and freeborn.

One of Isis's most important ceremonies, the Navigium Isidis, took place on March 5 to inaugurate the traditional sailing season; parades of priests, priestesses, and worshipers, all dressed in white linen and singing joyfully, marched to the seashore and launched a sacred boat. There were also secret ceremonies in which the participants reenacted Isis's search for and recovery of the body of her husband, Osiris. Because of the restrictions and monotony of their normal lives, for many Roman women these festive occasions—and many other aspects of religious worship—were likely moments to look forward to and fond memories to cherish.

Chapter 7:
Changing Lives of Women Under Christianity

No discussion of ancient Roman women would be complete without considering the beliefs and experiences of Christian Roman women, who by the end of the fourth century A.D. made up a significant proportion of the Empire's population. In the first and second centuries, encompassing the first few generations following the death of Jesus Christ, the Christians were few in number. They often set themselves apart from mainstream Roman society and practiced their rituals mostly in secret. This secrecy, combined with their steadfast rejection of the state gods and refusal to recognize the divinity of the emperors, made the early Christians suspect in the eyes of most non-Christian Romans. Members of the sect came to be seen as antisocial, a potential threat to public order, even as criminals. And the government persecuted them off and on for almost three centuries. The result was that Christians remained a small minority of the population even as late as the year 300.

Yet throughout the persecutions, the Christians persevered, and in the fourth century their numbers vastly increased. Even the emperors converted to the faith. By the 390s, Christianity had become the Empire's official religion. Non-Christians (then called pagans) still made up a large minority of the population, right up to the realm's disintegration in the late fifth century. Nevertheless, Christian beliefs and ideas had come to shape government policy, the law, and many social areas, including the lives of women and how society viewed women.

In retrospect it is easy to see why Christianity was able to make such phenomenal gains in so short a time, gains that profoundly affected the lives of millions of women. Mostly as a result of devastating wars, plagues, lawlessness, and poverty in the third century, the Roman populace had undergone a significant change of attitude. The old optimistic belief that Rome had been chosen by the gods to rule the world forever had been steadily replaced by feelings of hopelessness, despair, and apathy. Some felt that the gods they worshiped had abandoned them and, searching for comfort, embraced other gods, among these the Christian one. One aspect of Christianity that appealed to many, especially the poor and downtrodden, was its promise that everyone, including women and slaves, had an equal chance of finding salvation and happiness in life after death. As L.P. Wilkinson writes,

> [The Christians] brought to ordinary people of both sexes, often slaves, a simple and joyful message of love and hope that was not so novel as to be unacceptable or incomprehensible . . . hope of an eternity of bliss for believers as a compensation for the trials of this life. Their community was a haven for the lonely. . . . [They] were unique in transfiguring the sufferings of the poor [including most women, since most women were poor].[70]

Christianity's impact went far beyond raising the hopes and aspirations of the poor, however. The faith's rise to power and the spread of its ideals, some enlightened, others reactionary, transformed the attitudes and habits of a majority of Romans, including many women. In some ways the changes improved the lot of women. In others women found themselves even more limited and restricted than they had been before.

Changing Ideas About Sexual Behavior

Changes in attitude and habits advocated by Christian leaders permeated all areas of society. In the public sphere, the church increasingly came to condemn many traditional Roman customs, including gambling and attending the public baths, the theater, gladiatorial shows, wild beast fights,

A young woman faces death in the arena during a Christian persecution.

and even horse and chariot racing. These activities were characterized as sinful. Moreover, the practice of women baring parts of their bodies in the baths was especially sinful because it was liable to excite men and thereby encourage illicit sexual activity. In a work advocating the superiority of Christian values over traditional Roman ones, one of the early church fathers, Clement of Alexandria, admonished, "In no way should women be permitted to show any part of their bodies naked, lest both parties fall into sin, the men because they are excited by the sight, and the women because they attract the men's attention to themselves." [71]

Conservative Christian views, including those dealing with sex, also began to make themselves felt in various sectors of private life. The traditional Roman gods had rarely intruded into people's personal affairs. However, the Christian god, at least as portrayed by influential clergymen like the fourth-century bishops Ambrose and Augustine, was deeply concerned with the behavior, attitudes, and even the thoughts of individual humans. "Their sexual behavior seemed of particular concern to Him," writes classical scholar Charles Freeman.

It was perhaps at this moment that intense guilt replaced public shame as a conditioner of moral behavior. Ever more lurid descriptions of the horrors of Hell accompanied the shift. Soon consuming fires and devils with red-hot instruments of torture entered European mythology. [72]

In fact, to avoid God's anger and punishment, Christian leaders warned, women

Paul on Marriage and Divorce

In this passage (1 Corinthians 7:8–11), Paul, the early Christian leader known for his recruitment of gentiles (non-Jews) into the Christian ranks, encourages women to marry and discourages them from divorce.

To the unmarried and the widows I say that it is well for them to remain single as I do. But if they cannot exercise self-control, they should marry. For it is better to marry than to be aflame with passion. To the married I give charge, not I but the Lord, that the wife should not separate from her husband (but if she does, let her remain single or else be reconciled to her husband)—and that the husband should not divorce his wife.

and men had to drastically reform their sexual behavior. As Christianity's grip on Roman society grew stronger, people increasingly viewed women as objects of sexual temptation for men; female virginity became a treasured virtue; and sex, except by a married couple attempting to create children, became a sin. "It is well for a man not to touch a woman," wrote the first-century-B.C. Christian missionary Paul in the bible. "But because of the temptation to immorality, each man should have his own wife and each woman her own husband." (1 Corinthians 7:1–2)

For a long time, however, Christian leaders found it extremely difficult to convince Romans, even Christian ones, that it was wrong for a husband to have sex with women other than his wife. Roman men had been conditioned by centuries of tradition to think of such behavior as perfectly natural. In particular, they saw nothing to be ashamed of in having sex with their slaves. Even many early Christian wives agreed with and continued to perpetuate the Greco-Roman tradition of pretending not to notice such extramarital activities. (This was partly because a husband's sexual relations with a slave allowed a wife to space her pregnancies more comfortably.) But the church refused to budge in its attitude toward such behavior, condemning it as immoral. The fifth-century Christian writer Salvian asked,

A later European depiction of the Roman Christian bishop, Augustine.

What will the morals of slaves have been like when the morals of the head of the household had sunk as low as that? How corrupted will the slaves have been, when their masters were so

A Christian woman and her son worship in the catacombs, underground caves and tunnels where early Christians hid from the authorities.

utterly corrupt? . . . These masters didn't just provide a provocation to behave wickedly, but an unavoidable necessity, since slave women were forced to obey their immoral owners against their will; the lust of those in a position of authority left those subjected to them with no alternative.[73]

Female Submission and Devotion to God

Christian leaders did not confine their moral crusade to purely sexual matters, however. Practically any behavior or activity that appealed to a woman's vanity or brought her personal pleasure was suspect and discouraged unless it reflected on or glorified God in some way. The considerable time and attention Roman women devoted to their hair, for example, was roundly criticized; fourth-century churchmen repeated the words of an earlier Christian apologist, Tertullian, who lectured women:

All this wasted pains on arranging your hair—what contribution can this make to your salvation? Why can you not give your hair a rest? One minute you are building it up, the next you are letting it down. . . . Some women devote all their energy to forcing their hair to curl, others to making it hang loose and wavy, in a style which may seem natural, but it is not natural at all. [74]

The way a woman wore her hair did not matter, the argument went, since God was interested only in a woman's obedience, piousness, and good deeds.

As a further act of respect for and submission to God, Christian women were admonished to cover their heads with a veil or scarf when praying, an act seen as degrading for a man. Paul had earlier written:

Any man who prays . . . with his head covered dishonors his head, but any woman who prays . . . with her head unveiled, dishonors her head—it is the

Epitaph for a Christian Woman

This epitaph written by a man in praise of his dead Christian wife (quoted in Lefkowitz and Fant's *Women's Life in Greece and Rome*) dates from the late second or early third century A.D.

Her husband, who is still alive, has in his heart a memorial to his own wife after her irrevocable fate. Wayfarer, I have written this on a stone tablet, [a record] of what she was like. She had looks like golden Aphrodite [Greek goddess of love], but she also had a simple soul dwelling in her breast. She was good, and abided by all God's laws. She absolutely broke none of them. She has brought joy to her survivors. She began as a slave, but now has won the crown of freedom. She bore three live children, and she was the mother of two sons. After she had seen the third, a female, she left her life painlessly, on the eleventh day. She had an incredible beauty, like an Amazon's, to inspire passion more when she was dead than when she was alive. She lived simply for 20 years. This dark tomb conceals Macria Helike.

same as if her head were shaven. For if a woman will not veil herself, then she should cut off her hair, but [since] it is disgraceful for a woman to be shorn or shaven, let her wear a veil. (1 Corinthians 11: 4–6)

Paul justified this teaching by his belief that women were, by God's own plan, inferior, or at least subservient, to men. "For a man ought not to cover his head, since he is the image and glory of God," he said.

But woman is the glory of man. (For man was not made from woman, but woman from man [a reference to God's making Eve from Adam's rib in the Old Testament]. Neither was man created for woman, but woman for man.) That is why a woman ought to have a veil on her head. (1 Corinthians 11:5–10)

Moreover, in keeping with a woman's pious, submissive roles, she should be humble, quiet, and devote as much time as possible to contemplation of God. She should not presume to speak during religious worship, which was a man's privilege alone. Paul wrote,

The women should keep silence in the churches. For they are not permitted to speak, but should be subordinate, as even the law says. If there is anything they desire to know, let them ask their husbands at home. For it is shameful for a woman to speak in church. (1 Corinthians 11:5–10)

The fifth-century Christian thinker Pelagius advocated that women should set aside time each day for reading and studying the Bible. His contemporary Jerome even went so far as to suggest that marriage was, from a spiritual standpoint, an inferior way of living; it forced a woman to perform housework, child care, and other duties that distracted her from thinking about God.

Divorce and Remarriage

This heavy emphasis on sin and moral behavior naturally affected other aspects of marriage, including divorce and women's rights to pursue both marriage and divorce. Before the Christian revolution, Roman women had the right to sue for divorce at will and to remarry after a one-year waiting period. (By contrast, divorced men could remarry immediately.) Moreover, there was no limit on the number of times a woman could marry or divorce.

However, Christian leaders taught that marriage was a covenant between God and his earthly church and therefore not an institution to be taken lightly. Eventually the church said it was acceptable for a woman to remarry, but only after her husband's death, and only once, as third and fourth marriages were forbidden. Not surprisingly, divorce was seen as unacceptable. At first, these teachings did not stop Christian marriages from breaking up or many women

A Late Roman Divorce Law

This is part of the divorce law passed by the emperor Constantine I in the early fourth century (from Clyde Pharr's translation of the *Theodosian Code*).

A woman is not permitted to send notice of divorce to her husband because of her depraved desires, for a far-fetched reason, as that he is a drinker or gambler or womanizer, nor are husbands allowed to divorce their wives for any and every reason. But when a woman sends notice of divorce, only the following charges shall be investigated: has she proved that he is a murderer, sorcerer, or destroyer of tombs? If so, she is praised and recovers her entire dowry. If she has sent notice of divorce for other reasons than these three charges, she should leave even her last hairpin in her husband's house and be deported to an island for her great presumption. If males send notice of divorce, these three charges shall be investigated: do they wish to repudiate an adulteress, a sorceress, or a procuress? If a man expels a wife who is free from these charges, he must give back all the dowry and not marry another.

from seeking divorce, mainly because Roman law still allowed divorce. Christian leaders therefore urged their followers to live by a higher standard than human law. University of Liverpool scholar Gillian Clark explains: "In this instance they should refrain from divorce but concede it to a non-Christian partner, who might then remarry, although the Christian would not." [75]

The situation began to change in 331. That year, under pressure from Christian bishops, the emperor Constantine I passed a law that forbade women from seeking divorce for reasons such as adultery, physical abuse, or gambling. As stated in the law, the only grounds now acceptable for a woman were three extreme criminal behaviors by their husbands:

> When a woman sends notice of divorce, only the following charges shall be investigated: has she proved that he is a murderer, sorcerer, or destroyer of tombs? If so, she is praised and recovers her entire dowry. If she has sent notice of divorce for other reasons than these three charges, she should leave even her last hairpin in her husband's house and be deported to an island for her great presumption. [76]

The law also restricted men. Though they could sue their wives for adultery, that, poisoning someone and procuring prostitutes were the only acceptable grounds. The obvious double standard here was that women could not divorce adulterous husbands, but men could divorce adulterous wives. The church persevered to close this loophole, however. The late-fourth-century Christian preacher John Chrysostom wrote,

> Just as we [men] punish women who give themselves to others although they are married to us, so we are punished, if not by Roman laws, then by God. This too is adultery. The sexual act is adulterous not only when the woman is bound to another man. It is also adulterous for the man who is bound to a wife. Listen carefully! You may not like what I say, but I have to say it, to put you right for the future.[77]

Following this reasoning, in the fifth century the church repeatedly attempted to make divorce more difficult or even to outlaw it. Various emperors did impose further restrictions; however, they never went so far as to make all divorce illegal.

More Charitable and Equitable Treatment

Although the church's conservative approach to sex, marriage, and divorce placed certain restrictions on women's lives, women ben-

This European mosaic depicts the Christian preacher John Chrysostom.

efited, sometimes markedly so, by other changes wrought by the Christian revolution. In fact, many of the social ideas advocated by Christian leaders were concerned less with restricting personal behavior and more with making society more humane and equitable. And this was bound to have a strong effect on the lives of those treated most inequitably—namely, women, especially poor and unfree ones.

Christian preachers and teachers urged people to be humble, self-sacrificing, non-violent, and kind. Moreover, they insisted that such kindness should be extended to the realm's most miserable and desperate inhabitants—the poor, the sick, slaves, and even prisoners. As Christianity's ranks grew and more Romans accepted these ideas, providing charity to society's poor and powerless, so many of whom were women, became a large-scale, widely accepted activity. According to historian Averil Cameron,

> Already in the third century the church of Rome maintained some eighteen hundred widows, orphans, and poor by its charity; in fourth-century Antioch [in Roman Syria], three thousand widows and virgins were registered, quite apart from needy men. . . . The idea of giving to the poor was an important part of the Christian ethic, and such charity might also take the form of individual renunciation [of wealth]. . . . Wealthy Christians sold up their estates on a vast scale, giving the proceeds to local churches, making provision for feeding the poor on a regular basis, or giving them direct distributions of money.[78]

The Roman emperors, all but one of them Christians from the 330s on, reflect-ed these more humane attitudes in some of their social legislation. A striking example that significantly affected women was a ban on exposure (leaving infants outside to die). Since Rome's earliest days, fathers, through their traditional right of complete author-ity over their families, had routinely exposed handicapped or unwanted children. And strong circumstantial evidence suggests that many more baby girls were exposed than baby boys. Christian leaders condemned this practice; and they were instrumental in the passage of a law in 374 that labeled killing an infant as murder. (The law stopped short of declaring exposure itself to be murder because not all exposed babies died. Childless couples and others often res-cued and raised abandoned infants.)

Laws providing for more lenient treat-ment of slaves were another result of Christianity's softening effect on the harsher aspects of Roman institutions. Constantine passed a law forbidding the division of slave families during their sale, for instance. This kept wives and daugh-ters from being torn away from their fam-ilies, never to see them again. "A whole family of slaves [should] remain with one individual land-holder," the law stated.

> For who could tolerate that children should be separated from parents, sis-ters from brothers, and wives from husbands? . . . Take pains that through-out the province no complaint shall

hereafter persist over the separation of the loved ones of slaves.[79]

(Beyond these and similar measures, Christian leaders in the Empire's last centuries made no attempt to abolish slavery, but basically accepted it as a regrettable but entrenched and inevitable institution. Augustine recognized that slavery was evil in principle, for example, but he saw no alternative to it and preached that slaves would receive special rewards in the after-life for their earthly sufferings.)

Roman Women Transformed

With the spread of Christianity, by the Empire's end the beliefs, aspirations, and everyday lives of many Roman women were very different than they had been during most of the centuries of Rome's long existence as a nation. On the positive side, more female infants were spared and grew into young women, and many wid-ows and female orphans and slaves enjoyed better treatment. On the negative side, most women were unable to escape from unhappy marriages and had fewer legal rights than ever.

As for religion, the old gods and their rites were in decline and would disappear altogether over the course of the next few generations. Christianity had triumphed. And as barbarian invasions and other troubles caused the Empire to pass into oblivion in the late fifth and early sixth centuries, Roman women began their transformation into medieval European women. In time, they would forget the origins of their complex heritage, that unique combination of Roman and Christian values and customs that made them who they were. But they would embrace it and live it, from day to day and year to year, until, in the fullness of time, they had passed it on to the modern world.

Notes

Introduction: Roman Society's Unsung Heroes

1. Marjorie Lightman and Benjamin Lightman, *Biographical Dictionary of Ancient Greek and Roman Women.* New York: Facts On File, 2000, pp. xiv–xv.
2. Sarah B. Pomeroy, *Goddesses, Whores, Wives, and Slaves: Women in Classical Antiquity.* New York: Shocken Books, 1975, p. xv.
3. Pomeroy, *Goddesses, Whores, Wives, and Slaves,* p. xvi.
4. Diana E.E. Kleiner and Susan B. Matheson, eds., *I Claudia II: Women in Roman Art and Society.* Austin: University of Texas Press, 2000, pp. 1, 14.

Chapter 1: Early Roman Women: Legend Versus Fact

5. Livy, *The History of Rome from Its Foundation.* Books 1–5 published as *Livy: The Early History of Rome,* trans. Aubrey de Sélincourt. New York: Penguin, 1971, p. 150.
6. Elaine Fantham et al., *Women in the Classical World.* New York: Oxford University Press, 1994, p. 223.
7. Fantham, *Women in the Classical World,* p. 223.

8. Livy, *History of Rome,* in *The Early History of Rome,* pp. 43–44.
9. Livy, *History of Rome,* in *The Early History of Rome,* p. 99.
10. Pliny the Elder, *Natural History,* trans. H. Rackham. Vol. 9. Cambridge, MA: Harvard University Press, 1967, p. 149.
11. Larissa B. Warren, "The Women of Etruria," in John Peradotto and J.P. Sullivan, eds., *Women in the Ancient World: The Arethusa Papers.* Albany: State University of New York Press, 1984, pp. 235–36.
12. Quoted in Fantham, *Women in the Classical World,* p. 248.
13. Cicero, *For Murena,* in *Cicero: On Government,* trans. Michael Grant. New York: Penguin, 1993, p. 123.
14. Eva Cantarella, *Pandora's Daughters: The Role and Status of Women in Greek and Roman Antiquity,* trans. Maureen B. Fant. Baltimore, MD: Johns Hopkins University Press, 1987, pp. 122–23.

Chapter 2: Upper-Class Women Gain Rights and Autonomy

15. Pliny the Younger, *Letters,* published as *The Letters of the Younger Pliny,*

trans. Betty Radice. New York: Penguin, 1969, pp. 187–88.

16. Fantham, *Women in the Classical World*, p. 264.

17. Fantham, *Women in the Classical World,* p. 289.

18. Quoted in Fantham, *Women in the Classical World,* p. 334.

19. Even in later republican and early imperial times, children from most poor families were not able to attend school and usually remained illiterate; in fact, throughout Rome's history a majority of Romans were either partially or completely illiterate.

20. Quoted in Mary R. Lefkowitz and Maureen B. Fant, eds., *Women's Life in Greece and Rome: A Source Book in Translation.* Baltimore, MD: Johns Hopkins University Press, 1992, pp. 50–51, 53.

21. Sallust, *The Conspiracy of Catiline*, in *Sallust: The Jugurthine War/The Conspiracy of Catiline,* trans. S.A. Handford. New York: Penguin, 1988, p. 193.

22. Quoted in Paul G. Bahn, ed., *The Cambridge Illustrated History of Archaeology.* New York: Cambridge University Press, 1996, p. 300.

23. Tacitus, *The Annals,* published as *The Annals of Ancient Rome,* trans. Michael Grant. New York: Penguin, 1989, p. 184.

24. Quoted in Lefkowitz and Fant, *Women's Life in Greece and Rome,* p. 9.

25. Martial, *Epigrams,* in Lefkowitz and Fant, *Women's Life in Greece and Rome,* p. 169.

26. Seneca, *Consolation of Helvia,* in Moses Hadas, trans. and ed., *The Stoic Philosophy of Seneca.* New York: W.W. Norton, 1958, p. 129.

27. Pliny the Younger, *Letters,* in *The Letters of the Younger Pliny,* p. 152.

Chapter 3: Social Status and Occupations of Lower–Class Women

28. Pomeroy, *Goddesses, Whores, Wives, and Slaves*, p. 190.

29. Quoted in Lefkowitz and Fant, *Women's Life in Greece and Rome*, p. 17.

30. L.P. Wilkinson, *The Roman Experience.* Lanham, MD: University Press of America, 1974, p. 128.

31. Plutarch, *Life of Cato*, in *Makers of Rome: Nine Lives by Plutarch*, trans. Ian Scott-Kilvert. New York: Penguin, 1965, p. 147.

32. Varro, *On Agriculture*, in *Cato and Varro: On Agriculture* W.D. Hooper and H.B. Ash. Cambridge, MA: Harvard University Press, 1936, pp. 409–11.

33. Columella, *On Agriculture*, trans. H.B. Ash et al. Cambridge, MA: Harvard University Press, 1960, vol. 3, pp. 191–93.

34. Pomeroy, *Goddesses, Whores, Wives, and Slaves*, p. 193.

35. Lightman and Lightman, *Biographical Dictionary*, pp. 167–68.

36. Pliny the Elder, *Natural History*, in Lefkowitz and Fant, *Women's Life in Greece and Rome*, pp. 216–17.

37. Juvenal, *Satires*, published as *Juvenal: The Sixteen Satires*, trans. Peter Green. New York: Penguin, 1974, p. 136.

38. Tacitus, *The Annals*, in *The Annals of Ancient Rome*, p. 360.

Chapter 4: Women in Love, Marriage, and Divorce

39. Catullus, *The Poems of Catullus*, ed. and trans. Guy Lee. New York: Oxford University Press, 1990, pp. 73–75.

40. Musonius Rufus, *Reliquiae*, in Lefkowitz and Fant, *Women's Life in Greece and Rome*, p. 54.

41. Ausonius, *To His Wife*, in *Works*, trans. Hugh G. Evelyn White. Cambridge, MA: Harvard University Press, 1961, vol. 2, p. 181.

42. Pliny the Younger, *Letters*, in *The Letters of the Younger Pliny*, p. 161.

43. Pomeroy, *Goddesses, Whores, Wives, and Slaves*, p. 204.

44. Quoted in Lefkowitz and Fant, *Women's Life in Greece and Rome*, p. 20.

45. Quoted in Jo-Ann Shelton, ed., *As the Romans Did: A Sourcebook in Roman Social History*. New York: Oxford University Press, 1988, p. 48.

46. Catullus, *The Poems of Catullus*, pp. 59, 71.

47. Seneca, *de Beneficiis*, in *Moral Essays*, trans. John W. Basore. Cambridge, MA: Harvard University Press, 1963, vol. 3, pp. 155–57.

48. Ovid, *Love Affairs*, in Shelton, *As the Romans Did*, pp. 51–52.

49. Quoted in Shelton, *As the Romans Did*, p. 55.

50. Fantham, *Women in the Classical World*. p. 306.

Chapter 5: Women's Personal Lives and Habits

51. Aelius Aristides, *Roman Panegyric*, in William G. Sinnegin, ed., *Sources in Western Civilization: Rome*. New York: Free Press, 1965, p. 180.

52. Lightman and Lightman, *Biographical Dictionary*, p. xiv.

53. Soranus, *Gynecology*, in Lefkowitz and Fant, *Women's Life in Greece and Rome*, pp. 255–56.

54. Pliny the Younger, *Letters*, in *The Letters of the Younger Pliny*, p. 127.

55. Shelton, *As the Romans Did*, pp. 20–21.

56. Kleiner and Matheson, *I Claudia II*, pp. 8–9.

57. Kleiner and Matheson, *I Claudia II*, pp. 11–12.

58. Lucian, *Amores*, in Lucian, *Works*, trans. M.D. Mcleod. Cambridge, MA: Harvard University Press, 1967, vol. 8, p. 211.

59. Martial, *Epigrams*, trans. Walter C.A. Ker. Cambridge, MA: Harvard University Press, 1968, vol. 2, pp. 97–99.

60. Cornelius Nepos, *The Great Generals of Foreign Nations*, trans. John C. Rolfe. Cambridge, MA: Harvard University Press, 1960, p. 371.

61. Ovid, *Love Affairs*, in Shelton, *As the Romans Did*, pp. 352–53.

62. Livy, *History of Rome*, in *The Early History of Rome*, p. 34.

Chapter 6: Religious Roles and Rites of Roman Women

63. Fantham, *Women in the Classical World*, p. 230.

64. Livy, *The History of Rome from Its Foundation*. Books 6–10 published as *Livy: Rome and Italy*, trans. Betty Radice. New York: Penguin, 1982, pp. 319–20.

65. Livy, *The History of Rome from Its Foundation*. Books 21–30 published as *Livy: The War with Hannibal*, trans. Aubrey de Sélincourt. New York: Penguin, 1972, pp. 478–79.

66. Plutarch, *Life of Caesar*, in *Fall of the Roman Republic: Six Lives by Plutarch*, trans. Rex Warner. New York: Penguin, 1972, pp. 253–54.

67. Plutarch, *Life of Cicero*, in *Fall of the Roman Republic*, pp. 329–30.

68. Plutarch, *Life of Numa*, in *Lives of the Noble Grecians and Romans*, trans. John Dryden. New York: Random House, 1932, pp. 82–83.

69. Aulus Gellius, *Attic Nights*, in Lefkowitz and Fant, *Women's Life in Greece and Rome*, p. 290.

Chapter 7: Changing Lives of Women Under Christianity

70. Wilkinson, *The Roman Experience*, p. 196.

71. Clement, *Christ the Educator*, in Lefkowitz and Fant, *Women's Life in Greece and Rome*, p. 325.

72. Charles Freeman, *Egypt, Greece, and Rome: Civilizations of the Ancient Mediterranean*. Oxford, UK: Oxford University Press, 1996, p. 517.

73. Salvian, *On the Governance of God*, in Thomas Wiedemann, ed., *Greek and Roman Slavery*. London: Croom Helm, 1981, p. 179.

74. Tertullian, *On Women's Style of Dress*, in J.P.V.D. Balsdon, *Roman Women: Their History and Habits*. Westport, CT: Greenwood Press, 1975, p. 258.

75. Gillian Clark, *Women in Late Antiquity: Pagan and Christian Lifestyles.* Oxford, UK: Oxford University Press, 1993, p. 21.

76. *Theodosian Code,* in Clark, *Women in Late Antiquity,* pp. 21–22.

77. John Chrysostom, *Homily 5 on Thessalonians 2,* in Clark, *Women in Late Antiquity,* p. 39.

78. Averil Cameron, *The Later Roman Empire: A.D. 284–430.* Cambridge, MA: Harvard University Press, 1993, pp. 126–27.

79. *Theodosian Code,* in Naphtali Lewis and Meyer Reinhold, eds., *Roman Civilization, Sourcebook II: The Empire.* New York: Harper and Row, 1966, p. 487.

For Further Reading

Lionel Casson, *Daily Life in Ancient Rome.* New York: American Heritage, 1975. A well-written presentation by a highly respected scholar of how the Romans lived: their homes, streets, entertainments, eating habits, theaters, religion, slaves, women, marriage customs, tombstone epitaphs, and more.

Fiona MacDonald, *The Other Half of History: Women in Ancient Rome.* Chicago: NTC, 2000. Written for general readers, this volume presents a brief but informative overview of the lives of Roman women.

Anthony Marks and Graham Tingay, *The Romans.* London: Usborne, 1990. An excellent summary of the main aspects of Roman history, life, and arts, including roles played by women, supported by hundreds of beautiful and accurate drawings reconstructing Roman times. Aimed at basic readers but highly recommended for anyone interested in Roman civilization.

Don Nardo, *The Age of Augustus.* San Diego: Lucent Books, 1996; *Life of a Roman Slave.* San Diego: Lucent Books, 1998; *The Ancient Romans* and *Rulers of Ancient Rome.* San Diego: Lucent Books, 1999; *Greek and Roman Sport.* San Diego: Lucent Books, 2001; *Cleopatra.* San Diego. Greenhaven Press, 2001; and *A Travel Guide to Ancient Rome.* San Diego: Lucent Books, 2003. These comprehensive but easy-to-read overviews of various aspects of Roman civilization provide a broader context for understanding the leaders, trends, ideas, themes, and events of Roman history.

Jonathan Rutland, *See Inside a Roman Town.* New York: Barnes and Noble, 1986. A very attractively illustrated introduction to major concepts of Roman civilization for basic readers.

Judith Simpson, *Ancient Rome.* New York: Time-Life Books, 1997. One of the latest entries in Time-Life's library of picture books about the ancient world, this one is beautifully illustrated with attractive and appropriate photographs and paintings. The general but well-written text is aimed at intermediate readers.

Chester G. Starr, *The Ancient Romans.* New York: Oxford University Press, 1971. A clearly written survey of Roman history, featuring several interesting sidebars on such subjects as the Etruscans, Roman law, and the Roman army. Also contains many primary source quotes by Roman and Greek writers. For intermediate and advanced younger readers.

Major Works Consulted

Modern Sources

J.P.V.D. Balsdon, *Roman Women: Their History and Habits.* Westport, CT: Greenwood Press, 1975. Though dated in certain ways, this volume remains a sturdy, fact-filled study of Roman women that will appeal mainly to scholars and serious students of the subject.

Eva Cantarella, *Pandora's Daughters: The Role and Status of Women in Greek and Roman Antiquity.* Trans. Maureen B. Fant. Baltimore, MD: Johns Hopkins University Press, 1987. A commendable general introduction to ancient Greek and Roman women, with separate chapters on women in literature and in the writings of the philosophers.

Gillian Clark, *Women in Late Antiquity: Pagan and Christian Lifestyles.* Oxford, UK: Oxford University Press, 1993. This fine study compares the lives of Christian and non-Christian Roman women during the Later Empire.

Elaine Fantham et al., *Women in the Classical World.* New York: Oxford University Press, 1994. A very well researched, well-mounted collection of essays about ancient Greek and Roman women, with contributions by several noted scholars, including Sarah B. Pomeroy. Highly recommended.

Jane F. Gardner, *Women in Roman Law and Society.* Indianapolis: Indiana University Press, 1986. One of the best existing studies of ancient Roman women, this one covers guardianship, marriage, divorce, having children, occupations, female emancipation, and much more.

Peter Garnsey, *Social Status and Legal Privilege in the Roman Empire.* Oxford, UK: Clarendon Press, 1970. A general look at social classes in the Empire, with numerous references to women and their status.

Michael Grant, *A Social History of Greece and Rome.* New York: Scribner's, 1992. One of many volumes about ancient times by this prolific and thoughtful scholar, this clearly written general study is broken down into chapters on specific social groups, including women, freedwomen, slaves, the rich, the poor, and so on.

Judith Hallett, *Fathers and Daughters in Roman Society: Women and the Elite Family.* Princeton, NJ: Princeton University Press, 1984. A thoughtful, informative look at upper-class Roman women as revealed by the surviving evidence.

Richard Hawley and Barbara Levick, eds., *Women in Antiquity: New Assessments.* New York: Routledge, 1995. This collection of essays by noted scholars examines various issues surrounding the study of ancient Greek and Roman women and how the focuses of that study changed during the course of the twentieth century. Will appeal mainly to scholars.

Diana E.E. Kleiner and Susan B. Matheson, eds. *I Claudia: Women in Ancient Rome.* New Haven, CT: Yale University Press, 1996. A collection of enlightening essays on Roman women written by leading scholars in the field.

————, eds., *I Claudia II: Women in Roman Art and Society.* Austin: University of Texas Press, 2000. This follow-up to Kleiner and Matheson's 1996 book (see above) focuses on the portrayal of women in ancient Roman art, including paintings, sculpture, coins, and more.

Marjorie Lightman and Benjamin Lightman, *Biographical Dictionary of Ancient Greek and Roman Women.* New York: Facts On File, 2000. Very comprehensive and entertaining, this collection of short biographies of ancient women will appeal to scholars, students, and general readers alike.

Sarah B. Pomeroy, *Goddesses, Whores, Wives, and Slaves: Women in Classical Antiquity.* New York: Shocken Books, 1975. A groundbreaking study of ancient Greek and Roman women when it appeared, this is still an important and enlightening source providing an excellent starting point for those interested in in-depth further research.

Beryl Rawson, *Marriage, Divorce, and Children in Ancient Rome.* Oxford, UK: Oxford University Press, 1991. A useful discussion of female and family-oriented issues in ancient Rome.

Ancient Sources

Ausonius, *Works.* Trans. Hugh G. Evelyn White. 2 vols. Cambridge, MA: Harvard University Press, 1961.

Catullus, *The Poems of Catullus.* Ed and trans. Guy Lee. New York: Oxford University Press, 1990.

Cicero, *Cicero: The Nature of the Gods.* Trans. Horace C.P. McGregor. New York: Penguin, 1972; *Cicero: On Government.* Trans. Michael Grant.

New York: Penguin, 1993; and *Letters to His Friends*. Trans. W. Glynn Williams. 3 vols. Cambridge, MA: Harvard University Press, 1965.

Columella, *On Agriculture*. Trans. H.B. Ash et al. 3 vols. Cambridge, MA: Harvard University Press, 1960.

Dio Cassius, *Roman History: The Reign of Augustus*. Trans. Ian Scott-Kilvert. New York: Penguin, 1987.

Juvenal, *Satires,* published as *Juvenal: The Sixteen Satires*. Trans. Peter Green. New York: Penguin, 1974.

Mary R. Lefkowitz and Maureen B. Fant, eds., *Women's Life in Greece and Rome: A Source Book in Translation*. Baltimore, MD: Johns Hopkins University Press, 1992.

Naphtali Lewis and Meyer Reinhold, eds., *Roman Civilization, Sourcebook I: The Republic* and *Roman Civilization, Sourcebook II: The Empire*. New York: Harper and Row, 1966.

Livy, *The History of Rome from Its Foundation*. Books 1–5 published as *Livy: The Early History of Rome*. Trans. Aubrey de Sélincourt. New York: Penguin, 1971; books 6–10 published as *Livy: Rome and Italy*. Trans. Betty Radice. New York: Penguin, 1982; books 21–30 published as *Livy: The War with Hannibal*. Trans. Aubrey de Sélincourt. New York: Penguin, 1972; books 31–45 published as *Livy: Rome and the Mediterranean*.

Trans. Henry Bettenson. New York: Penguin, 1976.

Lucian, *Works*. Trans. M.D. Mcleod. 8 vols. Cambridge, MA: Harvard University Press, 1967.

Martial, *Epigrams*. Trans. Walter C. A. Ker. 2 vols. Cambridge, MA: Harvard University Press, 1968; and excerpted in *The Epigrams of Martial*. Ed. and trans. James Mitchie. New York: Random House, 1972.

Cornelius Nepos, *The Great Generals of Foreign Nations*. Trans. John C. Rolfe. Cambridge, MA: Harvard University Press, 1960.

Ovid, *Ovid: The Love Poems*. Trans. A.D. Melville. New York: Oxford University Press, 1990.

Pliny the Elder, *Natural History*. Trans. H. Rackham. 10 vols. Cambridge, MA: Harvard University Press, 1967; also excerpted in *Pliny the Elder: Natural History: A Selection*. Trans. John H. Healy. New York: Penguin, 1991.

Pliny the Younger, *Letters,* published as *The Letters of the Younger Pliny*. Trans. Betty Radice. New York: Penguin, 1969.

Plutarch, *Parallel Lives,* published complete as *Lives of the Noble Grecians and Romans*. Trans. John Dryden. New York: Random House, 1932; also excerpted in *Fall of the Roman Republic: Six Lives by Plutarch*. Trans.

Rex Warner. New York: Penguin, 1972; and *Makers of Rome: Nine Lives by Plutarch.* Trans. Ian Scott-Kilvert. New York: Penguin, 1965.

Sallust, *Sallust: The Jugurthine War/The Conspiracy of Catiline.* Trans. S.A. Handford. New York: Penguin, 1988.

Seneca, *Moral Essays.* Trans. John W. Basore. 3 vols. Cambridge, MA: Harvard University Press, 1963; and assorted works collected in *The Stoic Philosophy of Seneca.* Trans. and ed. Moses Hadas. New York: W.W. Norton, 1958.

Jo-Ann Shelton, ed., *As the Romans Did: A Sourcebook in Roman Social History.* New York: Oxford University Press, 1988.

William G. Sinnegin, ed., *Sources in Western Civilization: Rome.* New York: Free Press, 1965.

Suetonius, *The Twelve Caesars.* Trans. Robert Graves, rev. Michael Grant. New York: Penguin, 1979.

Tacitus, *The Annals,* published as *The Annals of Ancient Rome.* Trans. Michael Grant. New York: Penguin, 1989.

Theodosian Code. Trans. Clyde Pharr. Princeton, NJ: Princeton University Press, 1952.

Varro, *On Agriculture*, in *Cato and Varro: On Agriculture*. trans., W.D. Hooper and H.B. Ash. Cambridge, MA: Harvard University Press, 1936.

Virgil, *The Aeneid.* Trans. Patric Dickinson. New York: New American Library, 1961.

Thomas Wiedemann, ed., *Greek and Roman Slavery.* London: Croom Helm, 1981.

Additional Works Consulted

Books

Lesley Adkins and Roy A. Adkins, *Handbook to Life in Ancient Rome.* New York: Facts On File, 1994.

Paul G. Bahn, ed., *The Cambridge Illustrated History of Archaeology.* New York: Cambridge University Press, 1996.

J.P.V.D. Balsdon, *Life and Leisure in Ancient Rome.* New York: McGraw-Hill, 1969.

Anthony A. Barrett, *Agrippina: Sex, Power, and Politics in the Early Empire.* New Haven, CT: Yale University Press, 1996.

Richard A. Bauman, *Women and Politics in Ancient Rome.* London: Routledge, 1994.

Anthony Birley, *Marcus Aurelius: A Biography.* London: Batsford, 1987.

Sue Blundell, *Women in Ancient Greece.* London: British Museum Press, 1995.

Keith R. Bradley, *Discovering the Roman Family: Studies in Roman Social History.* New York: Oxford University Press, 1991.

———, *Slavery and Society at Rome.* New York: Cambridge University Press, 1994.

Averil Cameron, *The Later Roman Empire: A.D. 284–430.* Cambridge, MA: Harvard University Press, 1993.

Averil Cameron and Aemlie Kuhrt, eds., *Images of Women in Antiquity.* Detroit: Wayne University Press, 1983.

Gian B. Conte, *Latin Literature: A History.* Trans. Joseph B. Solodow, rev. Don P. Fowler and Glenn W. Most. Baltimore, MD: Johns Hopkins University Press, 1999.

T.J. Cornell, *The Beginnings of Rome: Italy and Rome from the Bronze Age to the Punic Wars (c. 1000–264 B.C.).* London: Routledge, 1995.

F.R. Cowell, *Life in Ancient Rome.* New York: G.P. Putnam's Sons, 1961.

J.A. Crook, *Law and Life of Rome.* Ithaca, NY: Cornell University Press, 1984.

Suzanne Dixon, *The Roman Mother.* Norman: University of Oklahoma Press, 1988.

A.M. Duff, *Freedmen in the Early Roman Empire.* Oxford, UK: Clarendon Press, 1928.

Donald Earl, *The Age of Augustus.* New York: Crown, 1968.

Charles Freeman, *Egypt, Greece, and Rome: Civilizations of the Ancient Mediterranean.* Oxford, UK: Oxford University Press, 1996.

Jane F. Gardner, *Being a Roman Citizen.* New York: Routledge, 1993.

Miriam T. Griffin, *Nero: The End of a Dynasty.* New Haven, CT: Yale University Press, 1984.

Harold W. Johnston, *The Private Life of the Romans.* New York: Cooper Square, 1973.

Robert B. Kebric, *Roman People.* Mountain View, CA: Mayfield, 1997.

Barbara Levick, *Claudius.* New Haven, CT: Yale University Press, 1990.

————, *Tiberius the Politician.* New York: Routledge, 1986.

Naphtali Lewis, *Life in Egypt Under Roman Rule.* Oxford, UK: Clarendon Press, 1983.

Ramsay MacMullen, *Christianizing the Roman Empire, A.D. 100–400.* New Haven, CT: Yale University Press, 1984.

Mima Maxey, *Occupations of the Lower Classes in Roman Society.* Chicago: University of Chicago Press, 1938.

Friedrich Munzer, *Roman Aristocratic Parties and Families.* Trans. Therese Ridley. Baltimore, MD: Johns Hopkins University Press, 1999.

John Peradotto and J.P. Sullivan, eds., *Women in the Ancient World: The* Arethusa *Papers.* Albany: State University of New York Press, 1984.

Stewart Perowne, *The Caesars' Wives.* London: Hodder and Stoughton, 1974.

Beryl Rawson, ed., *The Family in Ancient Rome.* New York: Cornell University Press, 1986.

Chris Scarre, *Chronicle of the Roman Emperors.* New York: Thames and Hudson, 1995.

Charles Seltman, *Women in Antiquity.* Wesport, CT: Hyperion Press, 1979.

Ronald Syme, *The Augustan Aristocracy.* Oxford, UK: Clarendon Press, 1986.

Susan Treggiari, *Roman Freedmen During the Late Republic.* New York: Oxford University Press, 1969.

Alan Watson, *Roman Slave Law.* Baltimore, MD: Johns Hopkins University Press, 1987.

Colin Wells, *The Roman Empire.* Stanford, CA: Stanford University Press, 1984.

K.D. White, *Roman Farming.* London: Thames and Hudson, 1970.

Robert L. Wilken, *The Christians as the Romans Saw Them.* New Haven, CT: Yale University Press, 1984.

L.P. Wilkinson, *The Roman Experience.* Lanham, MD: University Press of America, 1974.

Periodicals

Mary Beard, "The Sexual Status of Vestal Virgins," *Journal of Roman Studies,* vol. 70, 1980.

E.E. Best Jr., "Cicero, Livy, and Educated Roman Women," *Classical Journal,* vol. 65, 1970.

Mary T. Boatwright, "Imperial Women of the Early Second Century," *American Journal of Philology,* vol. 112, 1991.

D.E.E. Kleiner, "'Democracy' for Women in the Age of Augustus," *American Journal of Archaeology,* vol. 98, 1994.

Ramsay MacMullen, "Women in Public in the Roman Empire," *Historia,* vol. 29, 1980.

———, "Women's Power in the Principate," *Klio,* vol. 68, 1986.

A.L. Motto, "Seneca on Women's Liberation," *Classical World,* vol. 65, 1972.

Jane Phillips, "Roman Mothers and the Lives of Their Adult Daughters," *Helios,* vol. 6, 1978.

Beryl Rawson, "Family Life Among the Lower Classes at Rome in the First Two Centuries of the Empire," *Classical Philology,* vol. 61, 1966.

Susan Treggiari, "Jobs for Women," *American Journal of Ancient History,* vol. 1, 1976.

Elizabeth L. Will, "Women in Pompeii," *Archaeology,* vol. 32, no. 5, 1979.

Index

limitations on, 67
love and, 57–58
marriage and, 47, 57, 59–60
sexual exploitation of, 42
work of, 43, 67
Lucian, 75–76
Lucretia, 17–18, 33, 49

Maesa, Julia, 37–38
makeup, 75–77
Mamaea, Julia, 38
manumission (process of gaining freedom from slavery), 47–48
marriage, 54–62
Martial (Roman humorist), 33, 76
materfamilias (mother figure), 23–24
Matheson, Susan, 11, 72, 74–75
Messalina, 36
midwives, 69
modesty, 98, 100–102
monogamy, 54
morality, 64–66, 80–81, 98–100
Musa, 47–48
Muses (goddesses of the arts), 39

names, 14
Narcissus, 36
Nepos, Cornelius, 77–78
Nero (emperor of Rome), 31, 35, 45, 71
notorious women, 48

Octavian. See Augustus
Osiris, 95
Ovid
  adultery in the writings of, 63–64

flirtation in writings of, 79
mentioned as information source, 10
romanticization of women in legends
  and, 13
Sabine women in writings of, 16

paterfamilias (head of family), 23–24,
  42, 58
patricians, 83
  see also upper-class women
patriotism, 23
Paul, 98, 99, 102
Pelagius, 102
persecution of Christians, 96
plebeians, 83
  see also lower-class women
Pliny the Elder, 19, 77
Pliny the Younger
  childbirth deaths of women in writ-
    ings of, 71
  love in writings of, 56–57
  love letter to his wife, 25
  mentioned as information source, 10
  miscarriage in writings of, 70
  virtue and women in writings of,
    32–33
Plutarch
  adultery with slave women in writ-
    ings of, 42
  Catiline conspiracy in writings of,
    88–89
  mentioned as information source, 10
  scandal in writings of, 87–88
  Vestal Virgins in writings of, 91–92
Pomeroy, Sarah, 10, 39, 47, 57

Picture Credits

Cover Photo: © Araldo de Luca/
  CORBIS
©Angelo Hornak/CORBIS, 91
© Araldo de Luca/CORBIS, 20, 24,
  33, 34, 37, 51, 55, 90, 104
© Archivo Iconografico,S.A./
  CORBIS, 13, 40, 46, 52
© Bernard and Catherine
  Desieux/CORBIS, 86
© Bettmann/CORBIS, 68, 84, 95
Braun and Scnieder, 73
Bridgeman Art Library, 44

© Dean Conger/CORBIS, 57
© Francis G. Mayer/CORBIS, 32
© Giraudon/Art Resource, 19
© Historical Picture Archive/
  CORBIS, 27
© Mary Evans picture Library,
  36,105,83,89, 96
Northwind Picture Archives,11,
  17, 26, 28, 29, 41, 49, 59, 60,
  61, 64, 72, 74, 75, 78, 80,
  92,97,99,100
Prints Old and Rare, 15

About the Author

Historian Don Nardo has written numerous volumes about ancient Rome, including *Life of a Roman Soldier, The Age of Augustus, Rulers of Ancient Rome,* and Greenhaven Press's massive *Encyclopedia of Ancient Rome.* He is also the editor of *Classical Greece and Rome,* the second volume of the ten-part World History by Era series. Mr. Nardo resides with his wife, Christine, in Massachusetts.